Exquisite Behaviour

MAUREEN CAIRNDUFF

GILL & MACMILLAN

Gill & Macmillan Ltd
Goldenbridge
Dublin 8
with associated companies throughout the world
© Maureen Cairnduff 1995
0 7171 2245 X
Index compiled by Gloria Greenwood
Print origination by Identikit Design Consultants, Dublin
Printed by ColourBooks Ltd, Dublin

A catalogue record is available for this book
from the British Library.

1 3 5 4 2

For Mary who provided me with — A Room of My Own

Contents

Acknowledgments

My thanks to Michael Maughan, Wilson Hartnell Group, for kindly lending me a room in which to write, also to Mary Finan, Murrough MacDevitt and Barry O'Neill.

My gratitude to those who provided me with books for research — Mary Kelleher of the R.D.S. Library and Michael and Susan Colgan.

Without Deirdre McQuillan this book would never have started, and without the unwavering enthusiasm and professionalism of Eveleen Coyle it would never have been finished.

To my family, as always, I owe everything.

Introduction

'Manners are more important than laws. Upon them, in a great measure, the laws depend. The law touches us but here and there, and now and then. Manners are what vex or soothe, corrupt or purify, exalt or debase, barbarise or refine us, by a constant, steady uniform, insensible operation, like that of the air we breathe.' (Edmund Burke)

It was not these beautifully expressed sentiments of Edmund Burke that prompted me to write this little book. It was two unrelated incidents that took place within a few days of each other started me thinking about good manners and their relevance in society today, quite simply — how they affect our lives.

The first incident took place beside the footbridge that crosses the canal between Mespil Road and Wilton Terrace in Dublin. I regularly use the narrow, single file, footbridge as a short cut. During the morning rush hour the two-way pedestrian traffic can be quite intense. Often one has to stand aside to let oncoming traffic pass. All too frequently a furtive pedestrian slips in behind the one already on the bridge, doubling one's waiting time and one's irritation. One morning the stage was set for just such a performance, but instead of stepping on the bridge the young lady in question said, with a smile, 'After you'. I glowed with good will. A 'nothing incident' you might say. If only the day was made up of such 'nothing incidents' — the car that gives you space, the person who holds open the door when you are laden, the occasional 'thank you' — the world would be a happier place. The cliché, 'Good manners oil the wheels of society', like most over-quoted statements, is quite true.

The second incident concerns an obnoxious couple who created a fuss at a diplomatic dinner party because they did not consider their placing at table in keeping with the high regard in which they held themselves. Guests were moved and name cards transferred to avoid any further unpleasantness. When queried about it later, the ambassador's comment was, 'In my opinion people who count don't care, and people who care don't count'.

That set me thinking about those timid souls (unlikely to inherit the earth) who worry about doing 'the right thing', and the know-alls who steam-roll over them with never a backward glance. What exactly gives some folk the right to patronise the behaviour of others? What is this social chasm, sometimes referred to as 'good behaviour', which divides as cleanly as a knife through butter?

Good manners are not merely knowing what to do in given situations, they are first and foremost consideration of others. The socially insecure or rebellious may see manners only as an iron corset to constrain behaviour. 'Ah!' they say, 'what about using fish-knives, eating artichokes, introductions, R.S.V.P. invitations and all the rest of those confusing customs?' The answer here is that etiquette covers the traditional response to some unavoidable situations. Following the herd is by no means essential but to march to the beat of one's own drum takes a massive amount of self confidence, a sense of style and above all, the realisation that a choice is being made. For many, being out of step causes awkwardness and embarrassment.

This little manual offers a light hearted guide to the traditional methods employed in dealing with such occasions as births, deaths, weddings, unfamiliar sports, entertaining, as well as a glance at some still evolving customs concerning mobile telephones, the anti-smoking lobby, and escalator manners. It points out some of the pitfalls and derides many of the pretensions. In a time of social upheaval people tend to cling to traditional customs with all the tenacity of shipwrecked sailors clinging to flotsam.

Are manners inherent or acquired? Both in fact. There are some people, not too many, who put the feelings of others first, but the vast majority learn how to react to given situations. Oscar Wilde in one of his highly quotable flights of fancy declared, 'Nothing that is worth learning can be taught'. As with many of Wilde's aphorisms, there is more style than tennis — sounds good but is twaddle. Children can pick up the rudiments of good behaviour effortlessly, all they need is well-behaved parents.

Finally, let me dwell on the advantage of good manners concerning sex and revenge. First sex. Although not as potent as power or money, good manners could be termed a mild aphrodisiac, especially for women. There will always be masochists of both sexes but the majority react positively to care and consideration. Once upon a time there was an unspoken rule that gentlemen did not gossip. Nowadays even those in high places are rushing into print, the 'kiss and tell' tales making money but losing reputations. Rigid though the Edwardians were, it is with rueful amusement that I contemplate that classical anecdote regarding sexual discretion. A hostess throws open the library door to find a couple making love in front of the fire. 'Mending the carpet,' she murmurs retreating, 'how kind.'

Now for revenge. An example of the fine weapon that manners can be is given by the American author Judith Martin in her book *Excruciatingly Good Behaviour*. She points out, 'If you are rude to your husband's new wife at your daughter's wedding, you will make her feel smug. If you are charming and polite, you will make her feel uncomfortable. Which do you want?' Recently I drove to Dublin airport with a woman who has this scene sewn up. In the crowded car park, a car was pulling out. She moved in front to give more space, but her polite gesture was rewarded by one of life's charmers pulling deftly into the space. I was fit to be tied, she just leaned out of the window smiled at him and said, 'Sorry, was I in your way?' Abashed would not describe his face — she felt marvellous. If, on the other hand, any reader lacks the self-control for such exemplary behaviour, the chapter on Put-Downs might be of some assistance.

PART ONE

Entertaining

Making Introductions

I ntroductions can be a minefield, particularly for those who suffer from social amnesia, an affliction that affects us all at times. Provided that the name springs to mind, always introduce the less important to the more important. Thus, it follows that one should introduce men to women. For example, 'Mrs Bloggs, may I introduce Mr Brown'; slightly less formal is, 'Mary, do you know John Brown? John, this is Mary Bloggs'. The more casual and usual form is, 'Do you two know each other? Mary, John Brown. John, Mary Bloggs'. In the case of relatives, family comes first, 'Mother, have you met Mary Bloggs?'

An introduction to royalty, a Head of State, or a Very Important Person, is frequently referred to as a presentation — a term guaranteed to scare the socially insecure. The term is used because the formula is, 'Your Majesty/President/Minister or Very rich/powerful/talented Person, may I present Mary Bloggs'. (This Mary Bloggs gets around a bit.)

Let's have a look at some of the rules laid down for previous generations. Ward Locke and Company's *Etiquette for Ladies* instructs as follows: 'A gentleman must always be presented to a lady. When an introduction is made between a lady and a gentleman, both bow, but they do not usually shake hands. Often it is felt that a mere bow is uncordial and cold, and the hand is held out. It is not strictly correct, except in the lady's own house and should never be done by a man.' Time has loosened up this rigid formality. However, it is still supposed to be the lady who makes the first move regarding shaking hands or kissing. Try indicating that to today's social butterflies as they land kisses around one's aura — and yes I'm speaking of the men.

Custom dictates that the ranking lady presents her right cheek: there are single cheek kissers, double cheekers and even some treble kissers. On the whole it is a gesture rather than a kiss, sometimes more of a move forward, other times cheeks touch. The enthusiastic kisser touches lips to cheek, but if they are wearing lipstick they leave their victims carrying more war paint than an Indian brave. Kissing hands is a Continental custom and looks decidedly pretentious when incorrectly practised. Firstly, the man's lips should never really touch the woman's hand. Secondly, as in the custom of wearing tiaras, only married women have their hands kissed.

It is the custom in some countries to bow or prostrate yourself before dignitaries (a custom that many bank managers would be quite at home with). Good manners require that if failing to do this proves embarrassing for others, it would be wise to follow custom. A growing number, of which I am one, feel that in this day and age such obsequious behaviour is unnecessary. Respect should always be exhibited, but self-respect must be considered also. On this point the writer may differ from other guides in preferring to leave the degree of kowtowing to the discretion of the reader.

Introducing with a tag is favoured more than it is frowned upon. Certainly it can help immensely. For example, 'Mary, I would like you to meet John Brown who has just climbed Mount Everest. John, this is Mary Bloggs who takes a picnic to the top of the Sugar Loaf every Sunday', or 'Mrs Bloggs, may I introduce Mr Brown who has just moved to Ireland. Mr Brown, Mary is one of the most accommodating and entertaining women in the city'. In the first instance they can both launch into a mountaineering conversation, the second leaves plenty of room for manoeuvre. One confused, helpful hostess called Betty introduced two women who had not previously met. After the exchange of names she declared, 'You two have a lot in common'. 'Really,' queried one, an inattentive wife, 'what?' 'Your husband' was the brutally honest reply.

The flattering tag gets both parties off to a good start. A murmured aside that 'James is a tremendous admirer of yours' is a sure-fire winner. How can it fail: we all appreciate good taste!

The art of small talk is much maligned, yet it has much to recommend it, and nothing bridges those first awkward moments better. The world is full of people who boast that they are no good at 'small talk'. They belong to that same group, prominent at every cocktail party, who declaim that drinks parties are the dregs and usually they never attend. Who are they kidding? Lack of small talk indicates either boredom or stupidity, not qualities to brag about.

Shyness is frequently used as an excuse and like most social lies this can be taken with a grain of salt. The genuinely shy take care to practise the art of small talk in order to cover up their inadequacies. These brave folk are a different breed from those who imagine themselves superior to social niceties, and prefer to remain silent until they can shine in their own narrow field. If some folk won't make an effort, don't invite them.

As regards embarrassing moments when making introductions, social amnesia rates right up there with spinach on the front teeth or snapped elastic. The fact that it is so common makes it not one jot less embarrassing. The 'I'll forget my mother's name next' doesn't really work, better leave mother out of the excuses altogether. A semi-blank expression means one of the names springs to mind. Be thankful for small mercies and introduce the remembered name. 'You (whoever you may be) know Mary Bloggs, don't you?' At this stage the unknown should offer their name instantly. However they may not have read this book and only the very brave hang around on the off-chance of picking up the name, most folk drift thankfully away at this stage.

It is a commonly held fallacy that the American custom of repeating the name, as in 'Mary Bloggs, delighted to meet you', imbeds the name in their memory. Don't believe it. All it indicates is that for one second they got your name right. The test is to try them half-an-hour later while they are repeating other names around the room in the same parrot-like fashion. The only social group immune from this type of amnesia are politicians and it has been suggested that their ability to remember names is a very lonely virtue.

There are a thousand and one ways of covering up this social inadequacy. One is 'Darlings, you know each other' — not recommended for the clergy or politicians. All such white lies are quite transparent, and nobody is deceived by them, although the liar usually gains brownie points for trying. One school of deception swears by the well-worn lie where one admits to having forgotten only one name. When the forgotten one jumps in with 'Jane', the good liar bounces back with, 'Of course it is, I knew that, it is your surname that slips my mind'. This method is open to countless pitfalls, one of them being when Christian and surnames are interchangeable, such as Henry James. This method is only recommended for the very foolhardy.

To overcome the embarrassment caused by forgetting names, people who have met previously should come forth, hand outstretched, declaring, 'Hello Mary, I'm John' (only if he is though). Mary, practised liar that she is, will instantly reply, 'Of course I remember you'. John is flattered, Mary is relieved, everyone is happy.

The response to a formal introduction is 'How do you do', and the rather odd reply is 'How do you do'. To answer the question with facts or 'Pleased to meet you' may seem quite practical, polite even, but it is not part of the ritualistic formula. The usual response to make when re-introduced is 'How nice to see you again', whether it is true or not.

With complete strangers one starts from scratch. It is acceptable nowadays to introduce one's self. In the old days society was smaller and introductions less necessary as everyone was either related or acquainted. Some people still hang back until a formal introduction is effected, although this may mean losing an opportunity of making new friends. By today's standards being together under the same roof — at a house party, in the same club, university, or mental institution — constitutes an introduction.

Invitations

The Irish are not nearly explicit enough when it comes to invitations. If an American invites for a dinner party, one is left in no doubt as to what to wear (dress code they call it), where to go (directions frequently enclosed), what time to arrive and what to expect. If it is drinks at 7.30 followed by dinner at eight, it is clearly stated on the invitation card or over the telephone.

There is no doubt that we in Ireland are whimsical about time so it is therefore downright foolhardy to issue an invitation without stating the time. Asking someone for a 'bite at eightish' can mean, any time up to midnight for a sandwich or a six course sit-down dinner. Someone is bound to be disappointed.

A theatrical impresario relates being invited to the house of a friend of a friend. The friend said eight. The impresario, presuming a big supper party, arrived at nine to find friend and hosts watching television while dinner charred in the oven. Likewise, many a moderate drinker arrives at the appointed time of eight expecting to have a couple of drinks while waiting for the main event. Half-a-dozen gins and tonics later the poor sozzled guest realises that the expected intimate dinner is in fact a vast supper party with food being served nearer to midnight.

Dinner is dinner, supper is supper, and drawing a distinction between them allows guests to pace themselves. At the risk of spoiling life's little adventures it is best to be explicit when inviting. Give plenty of notice. A month would be sufficient for a formal invitation, a couple of weeks for a less formal one. Invitations issued over the telephone are best followed up by a reminder. (More about this under Acceptance, Refusals and Reminders, page 19.)

Format

Even the most casual have to face up to at least one formal invitation in a lifetime. It could be a wedding or a business function. Let's look at invitations and how to deal with them. The standard formal wedding invitation reads as follows:

Ann and Tim Smith

Mr and Mrs Joseph Bloggs
request the pleasure of
your company
at the marriage
of their daughter
Mary
to
Mr Jonathan Brown
at The Pro-Cathedral, Marlborough
Street,
on Tuesday 11th April
at 12 noon,
and afterwards at
The Ritz Hotel, Dublin.

R.S.V.P.
15, Thornhill Road,
Dublin 2

Wedding invitations should be posted out six weeks in advance (announcements are posted after the wedding, page 129). They are different in appearance from other invitations in that they are engraved or printed on the front side of a folded sheet of heavy paper. The invitations come from the parents, or parent of the bride. Additional marriage partners do not feature, otherwise the invitation card would read like a totem pole with scalps totted up on both sides. If a widow, or someone who wishes to deny the existence of a spouse is inviting, then only their name is used on the invitation. In the case of either divorced or separated parents, the mother's name takes precedence on the invitation in the United States. Over here it is reversed. Whatever the form used, if the natural mother is alive her name rather than a stepmother's is used. Inserting the mother's maiden name on the card gets the point across nicely. For example:

Mr Joseph Bloggs

and

Mrs Julia Mary Brown Bloggs

(the rest as above)

Equally, a separated couple may prefer to invite as:

Mr Joseph Bloggs and Mrs Joan Bloggs

Where the mother has divorced and remarried, the invitation could include the mother's first married name which, being the same as the daughter's, shows the connection. This is a matter of choice.

Mr Joseph Bloggs

and

Mrs Julia Mary Bloggs Murphy

If the bride is an orphan and the reception is hosted by a relative such as an uncle, then his name is on the invitation: Mr Frank Bloggs requests the pleasure etc. Wedding invitations are sometimes layered. Depending on the type of wedding, more than one invitation may be required. In the case of a small church or a Registry Office wedding, family and close friends only should be invited to the ceremony, with a large reception laid on for the other guests (the reverse is not on!). In this case two invitations are required, one for the combined church/ceremony and reception, and one for the reception only, making no reference to the ceremony. For example:

Mr and Mrs Joseph Bloggs
request the pleasure of your company
at a reception following the marriage of their daughter
Mary etc.

Post-wedding receptions are proving more and more popular as they are less formal occasions.

Avoiding a reception by holding the wedding abroad is also an option which is sometimes exercised when the couple have strong personal reasons to avoid a large wedding, such as a bereavement in the family, or when they merely wish to ensure maximum privacy. This may, however, be considered a bit parsimonious by some and unless there is a specific reason will be discouraged by all who enjoy a good day out.

Dress Code for Weddings

The dress code for weddings can cause problems. If it is a very formal morning wedding, morning dress is usually worn. This may be confined to the immediate wedding party (and those who boast their own outfit), while a lounge suit is quite acceptable for other male guests. An invitation to an evening wedding should carry explicit information: if black tie is expected, the invitation should make this clear. If the hosts omit any indication, do not be put off, simply telephone and ask. No matter how unconventional the wedding, the message should be clear. If a couple intend getting married on Ballybunion Beach in togas with a Roman-style orgy to follow, let the guests know what to expect. They cannot ever afterwards excuse their lack of imagination with 'If only I'd known', or 'My toga was at the cleaners'. Clear signals are good manners.

Twenty-first Birthdays and Other Celebrations

Anniversaries and twenty-first birthdays are other milestones marked with celebrations. The custom was that only the coming-of-age of sons was marked by pomp and circumstance, daughters being given a Coming Out party at eighteen. Etiquette dictated that it would be rude to identify a woman's age for all and sundry. For the life of me I cannot see how a Coming Out at eighteen wasn't worse, particularly if the guests for ever afterwards associated it with a twenty-first birthday.

Ann and Tim

Mr and Mrs Joseph Bloggs
have pleasure in inviting you
to a party for
Mary's 21st Birthday
on Thursday 1st July

R.S.V.P.
15, Thornhill Road,   *Dinner and Dancing 8.30pm*
Dublin 2   *Black Tie*

Printing

Paragons of good taste and those with money to burn consider engraved cards the only acceptable form for invitation cards. The rest of the world uses Thermographed or heat-raised printing — this is what gives the raised effect. The weight of the card is important, flat printing such as Letterpress or Litho working well on cards weighing up to 400 grams. Thermo and engraved printing can take cards weighing up to 600 grams; this feels like real quality!

The size of the card is as important as the weight and the print. Overcrowded cards look naff whereas a lone name in a large square looks a little pretentious as does a coat of arms or any insignia on private cards. Out also are gilded edges or rounded corners. Keep it simple, using plain black lettering on ivory cards with hard edges. I cannot think why, I am just following rules. An address, and not just a telephone number, should be supplied. We are only describing private cards here. None of the above applies to business entertaining: they can use or abuse the above suggestions. For them it can be more practical to give a telephone number.

Multi-purpose Cards

If frequent entertaining is envisaged, the simplest solution is to have 'at home' cards printed with your name.

At Home

R.S.V.P.

These can cover just about any situation. Underneath the 'at home', give the date, and on the bottom (opposite the R.S.V.P.) state the function and the time. It could be 8 o'clock, dinner and dancing, or drinks 6.30–8.30. If the invitation is to mark an occasion, this should be written between 'at home' and the date and could read: to celebrate John's 21st birthday, St Valentine's Day or whatever takes your fancy. (See under Luncheon, Buffet etc. for specific examples, page 138.)

There is an amusing tale told of 'at home' cards and the socially ambitious Laura Corrigan, a famous London hostess of the Thirties. Acquiring celebrities for her parties was a full-time occupation. Sending one of her cards to George Bernard Shaw, she informed him that Lady Corrigan would be 'at home' between 6.30 and 8.30 the following evening. The card was returned with the message — 'George Bernard Shaw ditto'.

Another popular invitation format is where the host's name is followed by 'requests the pleasure of your company', followed by the time and place. Both types of card can be personalised and bought in bulk, they will not date. Wastage could occur, of course, if the host or hostess changes name or address. A woman who enjoys a frequent change of partners would be well advised to stick to printing an address only, unless she is prepared to hand over the cards with the husbands. Elizabeth Taylor probably went through many a reprint! Cards bearing an address only could even be sold off with the house. Alternatively, most good stationers stock a blank card with 'at home' printed on it and you can then fill in the rest of the message yourself.

Feminists strongly object to the traditional form of wording on invitation cards as they invariably give only the hostess' married name. Feelings can overthrow custom on this with some couples using 'John and Mary Bloggs' or 'Mary and John Bloggs' and the entrenched insisting on 'Mary O'Brien and John Bloggs'. Single separateness in a business context is understandable but can be confusing when the couple is legally married. Fighting for a separate identity would seem to indicate a fear of being submerged.

Single hosts should give their name without embellishment. Titles are used on cards but not professional or honorary degree titles.

Addressing the Invitation

The invitation is addressed to the woman and issued in a woman's name. That is unless it is coming from or going to a man. The guest's or guests' name is hand-written at the top of the printed card, or in the case of 'requests the pleasure of the company of' it goes in the blank space provided.

Two weeks or ten days should be sufficient notice for a drinks party. If replies are required it is only reasonable to give a telephone number. Invitation by telephone is quite acceptable for an informal drinks party; in truth invitation by telephone is quite acceptable for anything these days, short of a wedding or a large dance. Whatever form the invitation takes it is only polite to reply if required. Numbers are an important consideration, particularly if caterers are employed and the hosts are charged by pre-arranged numbers.

Acceptance, Refusals and Reminders

Now let's deal with the much overlooked R.S.V.P. The English translation of *Répondez S'il Vous Plait*, is, quite simply, 'reply please', no reason for it to be in French at all! If no telephone number is given, a letter is required.

All formal invitations are replied to formally: Miss Mary Murphy thanks Mr and Mrs Bloggs for their kind invitation to the wedding of their daughter Mary at the Pro-Cathedral on Tuesday 11 April, which she is delighted to accept.

A refusal is equally formal: 'Miss Mary Murphy thanks Mr and Mrs Bloggs for their kind invitation to the wedding of their daughter Mary at the Pro-Cathedral on Tuesday 11 April, which she is unable to accept as she will be out of the country.'

Sometimes a reply card is enclosed with the invitation card. This demands very little effort from the recipient, merely a tick where indicated. There are even hosts who stamp the enclosed reply envelope. This is going a bit far; if one is fortunate enough to receive an invitation, the least one can do is answer it and post the reply.

Mrs Joseph Bloggs

at Home

Saturday 18th July

Drinks 6.30–8.30pm

15, *Thornhill Road,*   Pour Memoir
Dublin 2

The reminder can take the French form also — P.M. stands for
Pour Memoir or in plain English 'to remind'. If the invitation has
been issued by telephone a reminder card usually follows, and no
harm either as guests can be notoriously vague. Take the fellow
who turned up, resplendent in black tie, a day late. His exhausted
hosts informed him that the party had been the previous evening.
He apologised profusely for missing the event. 'You didn't,' they
pointed out, 'you were here. You enjoyed yourself and were last to
leave.' An exception? Perhaps. It is worth taking the precaution of
sending a reminder. The great thing from the guest's point of view
is that it doesn't require a reply.

'Regrets Only' has crossed the Atlantic and taken root here.
Not a universally popular import. It has its good points however,
being useful for corporate entertaining and large drinks parties. It
should not be used for private parties involving food and seating as
it can seem cold, impersonal, almost business-like, not at all in the
mode of old world hospitality.

Casual Invitations

Formal invitations are not an absolute necessity but they are a tried and trusted formula. Then there are the 'original' invitations, dreamed up by copy-writers, artists, wits or simply people who are sick to death of rigid formality. Indeed some of these invitations often turn out to be more entertaining than the party. They can take any form from sky-writing for the mercifully long-sighted to faxes for the time-challenged. Such gimmicks as a small cake with the invitation printed on top, a taped message or printed t-shirt have also been used. Many of these witty missives are for surprise parties.

The human race is clearly divided about the 'surprise party' — you either hate them or give them. A word of warning here on issuing invitations which quite clearly state 'surprise party'. It must be impressed on male guests that surprise means surprise and that they cannot bound up to the guest of honour declaring, 'So sorry I can't make your surprise party next week'. No need to warn women, they are accustomed to intrigue.

Formality is not essential for entertaining, far from it, but knowing the form is useful. Once known it can be disregarded. Not everyone is as formal as Mrs Ronnie Greville, a major bore on the English social scene between the wars. She pursued royalty as if they were the Holy Grail and her entertaining style was more formal than that of the House of Windsor. One of her complaints was, 'One uses up so many red carpets in a season'. If guests are made welcome and comfortable anything goes, except perhaps confusing business and pleasure, the personal and the public.

Getting in touch with guests takes time, but then nobody said entertaining wasn't both troublesome and time-consuming: giving pleasure usually is. Telephone contact with guests can clarify numbers, allow for replacements and identify dietary needs and personal feuds. It is best to steer clear of the latter — many a party has been drenched as opponents fire drinks across a crowded room. Bitter experience as an innocent bystander leads me to observe that as tempers rise, aim diminishes. On one such occasion I was standing innocently chatting with friends when two arch rivals spotted each other on either side of us. They promptly let fly with their drinks, throwing in their glasses too for emphasis. Not only were we soaked, we were nearly killed to boot.

Forewarned, it is no problem to cater for specific eating habits. No need to make an issue out of it. Not informing the hosts of special dietary requirements can cause embarrassment and is just not good manners. Remember — 'Politeness is like an air cushion: there is nothing inside, but it softens the shocks of life.' (Arthur Schopenhauer, 1788–1860)

Separation of Business and Private Entertainment

There are times when the fine dividing line between business and private entertaining becomes blurred. The successful executive with an impressive home naturally wants to show it off. Even if the company is picking up the entertainment tab and some of the guests are business associates, if the party takes place in the host's home the invitations should be issued from him/her, or his wife. Using a public relations firm is decidedly naff, and even using the host's own office is a bit off.

Most entertaining tycoons have social secretaries. These handlers help draw up the lists, order caterers, flowers and cars, whatever. Ideally they work from their employer's home but if they are in an office they should have a direct telephone line. It is a question of keeping up appearances. They should know the guests, how to pronounce and spell their names and where to seat them. To pass the organisation of a private dance, a wedding, a christening or other such occasion over to a public relations firm smacks of corporate hospitality and shows a lack of finesse on the host's part.

Good manners require that guests receive personal treatment. What George Bernard Shaw had to say about flattery applies equally to invitations: 'What really flatters a man is that you think him worth flattering.' Readers could counter that quotation with one from Dean Swift: 'Flattery is the worst, and falsest way of showing esteem.' Take your pick.

Setting the Stage

The greeting and the environment should put guests at their ease instantly. Warmth is the key here. Nervous, indolent and insecure hosts can be quite off-hand in their welcome. To recover from a cold start is all but impossible. Sydney Smith, the eighteenth-century clergyman and wit, described one of his hosts as having 'all the stiffness of a poker without its occasional warmth'.

Lack of warmth is not an Irish failing. We have a natural instinct for the welcoming gesture. All too often the insecure host fears appearing too effusive and adopts a sophisticated languor. Not a good idea.

It is only common courtesy to be on hand to greet guests as they arrive. Lying in the bath or peeling vegetables are not good enough excuses, whereas a dash to the local off-licence at least has the merit of extreme urgency. Butlers, footmen and Fort Knox timelocks aside, be on hand to welcome guests. Bonfires at the gates are no longer necessary to greet the traveller: a warm welcome is.

Monica was a frequent entertainer, a terrific but tardy hostess. Drinks were laid out and punctual guests were expected to fend for themselves. Accustomed to this casual style, Frank was not surprised to be greeted by a casual acquaintance when he turned up at Monica's for dinner. They chatted, and he was on his second drink when he remarked that Monica was late appearing. 'Actually,' replied the suddenly enlightened acquaintance, 'she lives in the same number house one terrace up.'

Tales of mistaken addresses abound in Dublin where it is possible to know most people, waiters included, in the houses of total strangers. Take Ann and James's error. They were bidden to Bill's house for drinks to celebrate the completion of a recent renovation programme. They arrived at the appointed time, and were greeted by name by the hired help. A quick glance around indicated that the renovations had been extensive, even the staircase had been moved. Our social couple mingled happily with old friends for over an hour, until a complete stranger approached and enquired who they were. Mellowed by the drink and convivial company they considered his query a bit abrupt, and told him so. 'Who do you think you are?' was the thrust of their reply. 'Your host' was his answer. Bill's party was next door and the staircase remained on the same side of the hall as before.

It is not only the welcome that must be warm, so must the environment. Nothing beats the glow of a fire in winter. Some hosts heat only the drawing room, one moves into the dining room to eat under threat of frostbite. There have been evenings when I have seen coats put back on at table. To have the house glowing and welcoming takes a bit of organisation, but not as much as you would think. One of the best tips gleaned over years of entertaining is to work backwards. Light fires, leave out ice, turn down lights, put on music and complete other last-minute tasks before the finishing touches in the kitchen and bedroom are embarked upon. It works.

Lighting the scene is of prime importance. Nobody can be convivial under the glare of arc lamps. Nothing equals candles for outrageous flattery. Never mind the mutterer who goes on about not being able to see what he is eating (they are inevitably male), dim lighting definitely brightens an evening.

'Seeing is deceiving, it's eating that's believing,' says James Thurber. A warm room, low lighting, scented air, soft music, sufficient alcohol, and good food will bring out the best in hosts and guests.

Arrival

Politeness dictates that ten minutes after the bidden hour is the correct time to arrive. Up to twenty minutes is acceptable, after that tempers begin to fray. On one occasion at a dinner where the ages ranged from eighty to thirty, the more senior guests arrived the acceptable ten minutes after the hour. One young couple breezed in over an hour late. By that time the first arrivals were on their third sherry and beginning to stagger. Good manners demand that even the unpunctual should be treated with warmth and eased into the company. This writer balks at this, feeling that if they have the temerity to arrive late they can shoulder a reprimand, otherwise they will go on their unpunctual way for ever.

There is also a time to leave (see page 78).

Flowers and Gifts

Time was when the only acceptable gifts originated from the donor's garden, kitchen, or needlework skills. A century ago, even twenty years ago, it would have been considered an insult to arrive at someone's house with wine, or any form of alcohol, let alone shop-bought edibles. In today's consumer-driven society all goods are welcomed in the manner in which they are given, as a gesture of friendship and gratitude. Although essential for a weekend stay, a gift is not necessary for a luncheon or dinner party, unless the celebration is to mark a specific occasion.

The begrudging donor may expect to share his gifts with his hosts. In truth, drinkable wine is often presented in the hope that it might replace the paint-stripper plonk that seasoned, but not immune, guests know to be on offer. It never does. Nor does the carefully chilled bottle of vintage champagne replace the interesting little apéritif from Sri Lanka. The pleasure is supposed to be in the giving.

To make the receiving of a gift also a pleasure is an important point often overlooked by even the generous-hearted. Just picture the pre-dinner scene: the hostess/cook/cleaner has given the house a thorough cleaning (quite unnecessary unless entertaining in full summer sunshine; candles flatter places as well as people, and even the most charitable enjoy a glimpse of the imperfections of others). Flowers have been bought at great expense and carefully arranged in every available vase. The mood is set. The kitchen surfaces and sink lie in readiness for the last-minute onslaught. The hosts are pink-faced with anticipation and perspiration. The door bell rings, the suppressed rush begins. On the threshold stands a beaming self-satisfied guest with an armful of cellophane-wrapped flowers. The gesture is generous but misplaced. The practically-minded will appreciate the gesture but mourn the timing with the house already awash with expensive blooms. Flowers sent a day in advance of the event will be really appreciated. Some people prefer to send the day after, to say 'thank you'.

It is often a good idea to enquire what the hosts would like. Marie went in for holistic decoration in her house, choosing flowers of the same type and colour. She was an all white tulip minimalist. In the crush of forty luncheon guests arriving simultaneously, only supreme good manners produced a warm 'thank you' to the donor of a tired bunch of orange gladioli. Plants in containers, or flowers cut with loving care from the garden of the giver, are a different matter altogether. Gifts from talented gardeners are always received with delight, although alas plants people are not notably generous with their hard-won bounty. Any item from the cultivated garden is welcome, be it cuttings, fruit, vegetables or flowers.

One open-handed couple in the fish trade were well-known for being generous with their produce, all of which was quite delectable, but there never seemed to be enough space in party-laden fridges for great wads of unfilleted fish. Think before you give.

Wine is another popular gift. However, taking a bottle of hooch to the house of a man with a renowned wine cellar is a foolish and pointless gesture unless the wine is priceless. A priceless gift is a bit over-the-top for a dinner party, or even a long weekend. Cynics would suggest that it depends on the hosts and a rule of thumb would indicate that the less a person needs the more he gets. The richer and more influential the host, the costlier the gift.

Kevin has created a reputation for himself as a giver of fine wines. Wealthy acquaintances receive bottles of vintage champagne, really powerful ones receive it by the case; his friends, who entertain him, remain giftless. Anyone intent on buying popularity should be prepared for a large outlay as one never knows when the overlooked may rise to prominence. Early slights bear long scars, and time wounds all heels.

Bottle parties are a different proposition. Even at these sometimes unruly events, a certain etiquette prevails. Basically the rule is — Do Not Be Mean. Drinkers should bring sufficient to satisfy their own needs. T., an established journalist who was known to enjoy a few drinks, and the last to leave a housewarming bottle party, had the grace to add a rider to her 'thank you': 'I brought a bottle and drank a case.' Quality has to be taken into account as well as quantity, in other words do not arrive with something you are not prepared to drink yourself.

Another problem can arise with those who insist on hiding their generosity under a bushel. These are the friends we all have who leave their unmarked, uncarded gifts on the hall table, a social category particularly prominent at Christmastime. Post-party clear-ups in some houses end up with a hunt-the-donor-of-the-parcel guessing game. Surely these must be the same people who year after year send Christmas cards with indecipherable signatures. 'Full many a flower is born to blush unseen/And waste its sweetness on the desert air.' (Thomas Gray)

Let's finish as we started — with flowers. U.S. Interflora coined the phrase 'Say it with flowers': most people follow their dictum. Flowers have taken over from the letter to express gratitude, regret, love, apology, congratulations or condolence. However, one must be careful about what one wishes to convey as flowers have their own language and in Victorian times were used as a discreet method of conveying messages. As only those with a Master's degree in Trivia would understand today's symbolism, it is best to include a written message also.

If every nuance of the following is lost on the recipient, they can still appreciate a genuine signature in your own hand. Contacting your regular florist and ordering an impressive bouquet is a lost opportunity unless a handwritten card goes with it. The sublimely lazy and far-sighted leave a stack of signed cards in their favoured outlet. There is no social etiquette for those who send flowers, usually roses, to themselves. They are probably the grown-up version of the youths who posted Valentines to themselves.

The Language of Flowers

Anemone — Lovesick

White Campanula — Gratitude

Red Carnation — Unrequited love

Pink Carnation — Woman's love

Red Chrysanthemum — I love you (this is a new one on me)

White Chrysanthemum — Truth (then there is the potted version)

Daffodil — Regard

Daisy — Innocence (meanness)

Fern — Sincerity (all the supermarket had on offer)

Forget-me-not — True love

Freesia — Friendship

Gladioli — Strength of character (lack of taste in my book)

Yellow Iris — Flame of love

Ivy — Fidelity (back to the supermarket again)

Jasmine — Sensuality

Larkspur — Fun

Lily — Purity

Lily of the Valley — Return of Joy

Mimosa — Secret Love

Orchid — Longevity (well at least they are longlasting)

White Rose — Truth

Single Rose — Simplicity (extreme meanness)

Red Rose Buds — Pure and lovely

White and Red Rose Buds — Unity

Sweet Pea — Au revoir (to summer?)

Red Tulip — Declaration of love (cheaper than roses)

Romantic young men who socialise within a small circle should be wary. Bruce was a young man about town. One of the wooing methods he employed was to send flowers. His florist recognised his degree of interest by the size and discernment of the order. To impress he sent armfuls of lilies (purity was the last thing on his mind); warmth was introduced at a later stage of the relationship with long-stemmed red roses (though why those scentless, scrawny blooms should signify passion is one of life's mysteries). Alas poor Bruce sent one bouquet too many: his latest love's lilies arrived while her flat mate's red roses were withering. In recognition of his interest in flowers the jilted lady sent him a wreath.

Corsages are extremely popular in the United States and are a compulsory purchase for adolescent escorts at debutante dances. In this writer's opinion they rate alongside plastic wreaths. For instance, where do you pin them? Some American corsages arrive complete with ribbons and feathers (I do not exaggerate), the wearer resembling a mobile Christmas tree. Simplicity is the keynote. Colour co-ordination is also important. It would not do to present an exquisitely simple purple corsage to the wearer of a scarlet dress. The popularity of orchids in a corsage has much to do with their longevity — they linger on as memory fades. Roses are fine but their life is even shorter than the event. Coolest of all is the snow-white camellia with its drop-dead Chanel chic.

The Dinner Party

'The best number for a dinner party is two — myself and a damn good head waiter.'

These sentiments expressed by Nubar Gulbenkian are fine for the very rich or for hermits, but the rest of us fall somewhere in between.

When it comes to entertaining, much the same preparation goes into a luncheon as a supper party, but as dinner is my preferred form of entertaining let's start with it. To create an effortless evening a great deal of forward planning is needed: organisation is the key to the enjoyment of hosts and guests.

The Guest List

If the occasion is to mark a family event or a career elevation the guest list will suggest itself. Well-mannered and experienced hosts plan a balanced list that will keep themselves and their guests entertained. This takes quite an amount of thought and trouble, but then nobody said being a good host was easy. The first step is to create the correct ratio between talkers and listeners, three talkers to five listeners being a good mixture. In Ireland finding listeners can prove difficult whereas in our neighbouring island the reverse is the case.

One star guest fills a table: two crowds it. Most stars imagine themselves to be great wits, in which case it is essential to deal with them in isolation: great wits, like great bores, recognise and avoid each other. A table could sustain a second star but a galaxy spells doom, as high achievers prefer to shine rather than be shone upon.

THE FLIRT

The type of woman who feels it's every man for herself plays an important role at the dinner table. She will keep the men on their toes and unite the other women, especially if she is the type who, according to Walter Winchell, 'has been on more laps than a napkin'. A little friction sharpens the wits.

THE BALLAST

The perfectly balanced guest who can talk as well as listen, and neither to excess. The problem here is that they rarely come in pairs. Moderation in conversation is a rare thing, particularly in Ireland. The Rev. Sydney Smith found Macaulay bearable company only because, 'He has occasional flashes of silence that make his conversation perfectly delightful'.

THE LISTENER

This brings us to the essential guest, The Listener. A word of warning here: never overdo the number of good listeners — a table-full is a very dull board indeed. While the listener concentrates on the speaker they are people of discernment and intelligence. Unfortunately, as Coleridge so amusingly describes: 'Silence does not always mark wisdom. I was at dinner, some time ago, in company with a man who listened to me and said nothing for a long time; but he nodded his head, and I thought him intelligent. At length, towards the end of dinner, some apple dumplings were placed on the table, and my man had no sooner seen them than he burst forth with "Them's the jockies for me".'

THE GOSSIP

The final ingredient to add spice to the mix is The Gossip. A little indiscretion goes a long way towards brightening up a dinner table: it can also lengthen the evening as nobody wants to be the first to leave.

The perfect mix is not always possible, inevitably there are long-standing friendships, social obligations, as well as, or including, the occasional bore.

THE BORE

Bores should not be inflicted on unsuspecting guests. This is where old friends come in, to help bear the brunt. There are masochists who feel obliged to have people at their table whom they thoroughly dislike — we are not talking of business entertaining here where the end frequently justifies the means — and this is not a good idea. If life is too short to stuff a mushroom it is certainly too short to endure antipathy, and at one's own expense. The only polite solution for this is never to accept hospitality one doesn't wish to return. Although it is neither necessary nor good manners to calculate on 'a cutlet for cutlet' basis, accepting hospitality does leave one indebted.

An horrific example of an unwilling and ungracious guest is the story told of Gilbert Harding (T.V. personality of the Fifties) who announced to the entire dinner table: 'I have been dragged along to this third-rate place for a third-rate dinner for third-rate people.' In the ensuing uproar he was forced to leave. Let that be a lesson on being careful with the guest list. A little drama never hurt an evening, disaster is something else.

It is still customary to have equal numbers of men and women at more formal dinners. Today's social freedom means that it is not always necessary or important to balance gender numbers when entertaining casually. A buffet supper takes care of this quite easily.

Pandering to what separates people rather than what unites them is not always the wisest strategy. Joan regarded herself as a progressive hostess. She specialised in inviting gay couples. For her the perfect dinner party was an equal number of each sex, but none of them heterosexual. The result was a nightmare of radical chic.

Forcing one's tastes on others is an error of judgment and a lapse of good manners. Michael, who ran a chain of Dublin shoe shops in the Seventies, had a one-legged customer, a man who bought size nine shoes and threw away the right one. Well-intentioned Michael became obsessed with the Cinderella mission of finding a right foot to fit the other shoe. Eventually he did. He was thrilled, but not his one-legged customers; they didn't have the same taste and couldn't agree on style!

Filling a dinner table with a single-interest group can create difficulties, not least for the partners who have heard all the legal, medical, political, golfing and sailing stories before. A virgin audience is one of life's more generous offerings.

Table Placing

The French word *placement* quite simply means table placing. For the more formal meals there will be a seating plan on view at the entrance. Although a laid-out table plan sounds rather pretentious, and in a private house it is a little, it does mean that once you have read the seating plan you can save your dinner companions for the table and spread your pearls of wisdom among the other guests during pre-dinner drinks. It also offers an opportunity to make a few discreet enquiries if one is to be seated beside unknowns. If one has no idea what sort of an evening to expect, it is not a bad idea to ask if there will be *placement*, in which case a late arrival or a 'no show' is in serious trouble. The less formal *placement* is a name card at each table place, even less formal is when the plan remains in the host's head. The purpose behind the *placement* is not to give the hosts the choicest morsels on the guest list. It is to ensure that the Most Important People sit at the head of the table, or beside the hosts, and to regulate the remainder according to their status in the eyes of society — a procedure known as Order of Precedence. A guideline for what could be perceived as status in the eyes of the Republic is given below.

The President of Ireland
Cardinals
Prime Minister
Members of the Cabinet — Ministers
Apostolic Nuncio
Ambassadors
The Archbishop
Plenipotentiary Ministers
The Bishop
The Chief Justice
Speakers of Parliament
Head of Senate
The President of the High Court
The Attorney General
The Council of State
Judges of the Supreme Court
Judges of the High Court
Chargé d'Affaires
Parliamentary Secretaries
Lord Mayor of Dublin
ex Ministers
Circuit Court Judges
Deputies and Senators
Heads of Government Departments
Chief of Staff (Army)
Chief of Police

A word of consolation for readers who have searched in vain for their inclusion in the above list. It is often preferable, certainly more fun, to be seated 'below the salt' as that social Siberia far from the V.I.P.s is known.

The Luncheon Party

'All that I ever ask of my friends is that they survive until lunchtime.' (Noël Coward)

As one gets older luncheon takes on a different aspect. For the young it is a necessary bite in the middle of the day. A few years on it means a social or rushed break from the office. For the slightly older, who are by now 'doing lunch', a lunch date could be the beginning of an affair. The luncheon table is about the only place where married folk can smoulder. Lunch can also mean relaxed, boozy weekend meals — the long lunches' journey into night. There is too that highly indigestible meal, the business lunch, but selling a deal is not the ideal aid to digestion. This writer is of the opinion that offices are for business and mealtimes are for relaxation. Finally, in those golden years, luncheon joins the funeral as the most enjoyable event of the social calender.

Luncheon Fare

The very first luncheon party I gave was nearly ruined for me when one of my guests pointed out that 'one did not serve soup at luncheon'. It was summer and I had slaved over vichyssoise. To say that I was devastated would be untrue but I was certainly put out. Then the thought occurred 'how dare the little so-and-so try to ruin my party and tell me what to do', a sentiment which you, gentle reader, may be all too aware of by now, but bear in mind that this writer does not intend to put down, only to point out life's little pitfalls. Such was not the motive of the the no-soup-at-luncheon guest. Serve soup if you want, it may be a food that is more suited to the evening, but it's your party and you can do what you want. Your guests are fortunate indeed to be invited. Therefore luncheon food, in common with all other meals, is what the host chooses to serve. Having said that, it is a bit unfair to serve mid-week working guests a heavy game dish accompanied by a full-bodied red wine. This is evening fare, a meal to linger over and digest in comfort. Luncheon food is best kept light.

Punctuality

As always punctuality is to be expected. It is essential at this early hour of the day. Business lunches dictate their own time, whatever fits into crowded schedules. Press luncheons, viewed from a journalist's point of view, have the irritating habit of running late. Organisers blame the press, saying they never turn up on time, the press insist that if they do they have to hang around for hours. If presentations were prompt everyone would be fed and watered on time and ready to go about their business. Far too often the importance of the event to the organisers blinds them to the schedules of others.

Luncheon Invitations

'At home' cards can be used for lunch, dinner, drinks and other invitations. The format would run something like this

---

Tim and Anne

Mr and Mrs Joseph Bloggs

at Home

Saturday 4th July

R.S.V.P.
15, Thornhill Road,
Dublin 2

Luncheon

1 p.m.

Buffets

Sitting down to a meal is one of life's few legitimate pleasures. Standing with a plate in one hand and a glass in the other is a penance. However pleasure often perishes on the altar of convenience, mobility and numbers. The simple truth is that buffet meals 'get rid' of the maximum number of guests at minimal cost. A standing buffet does not encourage guests to linger over their food and drink.

To realise just how awkward a buffet meal can be one would have to see the fix that Ian got himself into at a large housewarming buffet luncheon party. His first fall from grace occurred in the newly-painted drawing room when his harrassed host thrust a bottle of champagne at him and asked him to open it. No problem for Ian who was a dab hand at removing corks from bottles. As he removed the wire someone asked him directions to the bathroom. In swinging around to point the way he dislodged the cork and sprayed the newly painted walls with golden bubbles. 'I'm so sorry,' he said abjectly to the host. 'And well you might be' was the ungracious reply.

His next faux-pas took place in the dining room. Here he collected his full plate and glass and positioned himself out of harm's way in a quiet corner. As he relaxed against the wall he felt a painting, which he hadn't noticed, unhook itself and lodge on his shoulders. There he stood, ramrod straight, plate in one hand, cutlery and glass in the other, and a painting on his shoulders. After about twenty minutes he finally caught his wife's eye and she came and rescued him. The afternoon was drawing to a close without further mishap when the children of the house invited him to climb out the window and join them in a game. The low window presented no problems, unfortunately as he swung his legs down on the other side, he caught his foot in a creeper and ripped it off the wall. He went straight to his car. Poor man, had he been seated at a table none of this would have happened.

THE ADVANTAGES

Of course buffet entertaining is not all bad. A well-organised buffet with suitable food and adequate seating is hard to beat. The carefully thought-out buffet provides tables and chairs. There may even be *placement*, or table placing. Almost as bad as attempting the balancing act on foot is the 'seat only' balancing act. Here, although you have the weight off your feet, you still have to contend with a plate on your knee and a glass at your feet. Frequently, this hard-won seat is one in a line against a wall, a position guaranteed to make even the most sought-after party person feel like a wallflower in *Ballroom of Romance*. To join in conversation one has to shout upwards at the group still standing. This never works, the standing party having by now formed their own exclusive chairless club. Another place to perch is the stairs even if it means constantly getting up to clear passageway as well as offering those on the steps beneath an unhindered view of underwear.

The best buffet meals are those where tables and chairs are provided. A common error is squashing in as many people as possible. Entertaining is supposed to be enjoyable.

Here are some advantages of the buffet:

- easier to prepare in advance
- requires no waiters
- can accommodate more people
- less demanding in terms of *haute cuisine*
- usually means only one course and pudding
- can accommodate odd numbers of guests, and even lose a few 'odd' guests

- can be more fun, more casual and relaxed
- can cater for different tastes
- are an ideal setting in which to move around and meet people.

BUFFET INVITATIONS

Invitations to a buffet are less formal than to a dinner. Once again 'at home' cards are ideal. For a buffet it is quite correct only to state the time.

BUFFET WEDDINGS

Completely stand-up weddings are more common in the U.K. than they are in Ireland. Maybe their expectations of wedding hospitality are more limited. A reception can consist of a vol-au-vent, a couple of sausages, two or three glasses of bubbly, and a leave-your-present-and-on-your-way attitude. However, meanness is a sin in Ireland and fear of sinking to such ignominy forces many a father of the bride into bankruptcy. The ideal arrangement for this two-families-and-friends ritual is a buffet with table, chairs and table placing. The freer atmosphere of the buffet allows the younger guests to mingle more easily after the meal is over, while the older guests have the security of their given places.

BUFFET FOOD AND LAYOUT

The obvious is often ignored with buffet food — that being that it must be easy to eat. This applies particularly to standing-only buffets. Well-chosen food for this occasion is the type that even the clumsiest can manage. That means avoiding any foods that need cutting, or that shoot across the plate. For some illogical reason cold meats and salads are popular stand-up foods. I defy anyone to cut up slices of ham and leaves of lettuce while standing. Finely-shredded lettuce and bite-sized morsels of meat are a different proposition.

Suitable foods are mushy, not runny, lasagne rather than meat and gravy. Buttered rolls are better than baskets of bread and plates of butter. Convenience can be married to taste. Waves of antipathy sweep over me when I encounter the catered and served buffet where the staff ration all one's favourite dishes, even being miserly with the boiled rice. A buffet must be splendid.

Ideally the serving table should be a picture, a still life with whole fish, fowl, legs of lamb, loins of beef, even suckling pig. A meal with a mediaeval air of plenty. Clearly there is no need to serve any of the above, but whatever is served should be in abundance and the table prettily decorated with flowers. It is not a good idea to skimp on time and money by using disposable plates and cutlery. Paper napkins are acceptable to most people today (but not to me) whereas paper plates and plastic cutlery are not.

Placing the buffet for the maximum convenience of guests is important. Two buffet tables at separate ends of a large room divide a crowd neatly; long tables with identical dishes at either end and plates and cutlery in the middle is another good solution. It can work also with a round table where duplicate dishes are arranged on either side and plates in the centre. Easy access avoids painful queueing.

If at all possible, it is best not to lay out puddings and cheeses at the same time as the main course. They are an irresistible attraction for the short-sighted and the greedy. The former confuse custard with mayonnaise and tart with quiche and end up with a plate filled with sweet and sour. The latter demolish the cheese with their meat, fish and salad. A separate table for the second course lessens the confusion and to clear and replace avoids it altogether.

At a seated buffet the guests are frequently served pudding and coffee at the table, which suits those replete guests too engrossed in conversation or too Brahms and Lizst to help themselves further.

BUFFET ETIQUETTE

Polite people remember when they reach the serving table that they are in a private house and not an eat-as-much-as-you-can-for £££ restaurant. They do not heap their plates in an attempt to get their money's worth. The super polite will take only small portions of one or two dishes and return for more as they feel like it. They are probably the same people who offer to help other guests at the table. Not only are their manners to be admired, but their slim figures too. Although buffet meals afford gregarious guests an opportunity to move around, too many changes of place can look ill-mannered, even unstable.

Breakfast and Brunch

'In England people actually try to be brilliant at breakfast. That is so dreadful of them! Only dull people are brilliant at breakfast.' (Oscar Wilde)

Breakfast entertaining should be reserved for two consenting adults only and the ideal location is a large bed. The United States have given us (quite unnecessarily) the Power Breakfast. At the Power Breakfast vast amounts of delicious food such as fish, grilled bacon, sausages, tomatoes and eggs are allowed to congeal while high-powered executives, ties thrown over their shoulders, get revved up for their business day. What do these power brokers start their day on? Nothing is usually the answer. A heavy 'breakfast' might be orange juice and coffee; decent breakfast food is wasted on them. There is a school of thought (of which this writer is an eager pupil) that insists that Power Breakfasts are a waste of time.

There are no special invitations for breakfast, other than a murmur or a summons. Dressing, or undressing for the occasion depends on the location.

BRUNCH

Brunch is another transatlantic import, but a civilised one. A weekend brunch permits weekday workers to socialise and still retain most of the day for themselves. Breakfast ruins a lie-in and lunch can be an all-day session.

There is no special etiquette for brunch, all that is required is to arrive on time, to leave (hopefully) before dark, and to enjoy the party. Dress is casual.

SUITABLE FOOD AND DRINK

Brunch food depends on the numbers and the help available. It is not a meal to prepare in advance. Smoked salmon and scrambled eggs are perennial favourites, as are omelettes but cooked eggs must be eaten immediately. Grilled traditional breakfast foods such as bacon, sausage, black pudding, and kidneys wait a little better for late arrivals. Kedgeree or a creamed chicken dish can hang around indefinitely. All the calorie laden foods such as fried bread, French toast, croissants and sweet rolls are wolfed down with proper, as opposed to instant, tea and coffee.

A simple easy-to-serve drink on such an occasion is Buck's Fizz (known as Mimosa in the U.S.). Decent sparkling wine can take the place of champagne, but the orange juice must be top quality, either freshly squeezed or one of the better frozen brands. Bloody Marys are another good kick-start to the day, and go best with the more solid grilled foods. Vodka mixes are light and effective; Screwdrivers consist of orange juice with vodka and Bull Shots are vodka with bouillon (see Cocktails, page 53). Bull Shot drinkers are usually in recovery or anticipation, and as the drink has both nourishment and kick they often drink their brunch.

Sunday Brunches in restaurants have taken off in a big way, and are especially attractive to the unmarried. Sunday newspapers and a general air of indolence give them a relaxed holiday feeling.

The Cocktail Party

'Cocktail parties are the worst invention since castor oil.' (Elsa Maxwell)

Elsa Maxwell was a rather unattractive P.R. lady of the Forties and Fifties, famous for throwing immense, and highly publicised parties at other people's expense. According to her, cocktail parties were merely a way of paying back second-hand debts and entertaining people you wouldn't invite for dinner. Well, if the expense of a big dinner party was not yours, you would say that wouldn't you?

She is not alone in holding this view — 90% of the people one meets at cocktail parties profess to be of the same opinion. Why then are they there? Politeness perhaps, but more likely curiosity, or quite frequently to offer living proof that they were invited. Other forms of entertaining may be more fulfilling but drinks parties (hardly anyone refers to them as cocktail parties these days) are ideal for a preliminary social skirmish. For the unattached they serve as an introduction or dating agency, so hosts are actually performing an important social service. Many of the already attached become semi or totally detached as the result of a chance meeting over drinks.

From a host's point of view drinks parties are indeed a way of paying back hospitality, not necessarily to those you wouldn't invite to dinner, but to a broader and more adventurous cross-section than might suit a modest dinner table. Then again, some hosts never indulge in any other form of entertaining, so one should be grateful for small mercies.

It is claimed repeatedly that if hosts enjoy their own party, it cannot have been a good one. This is nonsense! Of course hosts should enjoy themselves. The guests, after all, were their selection so it goes without saying that none should be ignored. The best hosts are the ones who actually enjoy being hosts.

Preparation

It is important to ensure that the supply of the essential ingredient at a drinks party will be greater than the demand. Running out of alcohol makes a host appear mean. Shortage of food at a dinner party is certainly worse, but rarer. Buying on a 'sale or return' basis from an off-licence is the wisest move. Reputable wine merchants might charge a bit more but they can usually arrange the hire of glasses and waiters also.

Ice is the second most important ingredient at a drinks party. Forward planners, or those without an ice-making machine or the opportunity to buy ice, build up a store by emptying the ice from the trays into plastic bags for days before the party. On the night, all the bag needs is a hard knock to separate the cubes.

THE GLASSES

Next come glasses, the most common variety on offer at most parties being those inhospitable ones, slightly larger than sherry glasses. When ice is added the contents amount to one decent swallow. Glasses of this size do not reduce the amount of alcohol drunk, they merely double the waiter's work. Mixed drinks, such as whiskey and water or gin and tonic should come in a generous-sized glass, not a beer glass: a large stemmed one or a wide based tumbler fills the bill nicely.

Forget the assumption that drinks parties need next to no preparation — what you put into a party shows. Any successful party takes time and effort, the essential ingredient being the right mix of people, enough to drink, and a warm relaxed atmosphere.

HIRING HELP

If the number invited exceeds twenty, you may need help. As already mentioned a good wine merchant or off-licence often supply the names of reputable waiters. One waiter can cope with about fifty guests provided he knows the numbers expected and what to serve, and provided he does not over-indulge himself. In London, the smartest parties boast actors pretending to be drunken waiters. This works as an ice breaker for our more reserved neighbours but it has been tried here without success. Nobody noticed.

On a personal note, my husband has looked after the bar at our drinks parties over the years. One organised person can do wonders. He served from a small but well laid-out drinks trolley where everything he needed was at hand; he also had the advantage of knowing how our friends like their drinks. However in the interests of marital unity it might be as well to hire help, especially if, like him, you are married to a compulsive inviter. As the trolley was set up the same conversation ensued prior to every party — and there were many. He would enquire, 'How many are invited?' The mumbled reply was never clear. He would then ask for a few names and when the litany exceeded fifty he would say, 'Right I'll serve the first fifty and no more.' The numbers frequently exceeded 100, but he never carried out his threat — thank goodness!

DRINKS

For those with unlimited budgets there is no doubt that serving champagne simplifies a drinks party. However after a long, tiring day at the office it may not be what every guest wants. Many an exhausted executive looks forward to relaxing with a glass of their favourite tipple. Leaving aside the all-champagne diet, the essential drinks are white wine, and three spirits such as whiskey, gin and vodka, mixers, plenty of bottled water and a good non-alcoholic drink.

For pre-luncheon drinks parties, champagne is excellent, either straight or mixed with orange juice. As already mentioned the champagne can be replaced by sparkling wine but the juice must be first-rate, either freshly squeezed or top quality frozen. Vodka and tomato juice (Bloody Mary) or vodka and consommé (Bull Shot) are fast working pick-me-ups; vodka and orange juice (Screwdriver) is another fast action hair-of-the-dog. In summertime it is hard to beat a long cool Pimms; this should be made to the correct strength — one measure of Pimms to three of lemonade, topped up with half the kitchen garden.

A heavy hand with some of the above drinks is dangerous, particularly the easy-to-down Pimms. One generous-hearted hostess, called M. invited some women friends for luncheon and to watch one of the royal weddings on television. With the intention of getting the 'girls' to relax she spiked the Pimms with a half bottle of poteen. Instead of getting the party going, within minutes her guests were paralysed; lunch was forgotten as black coffee was used as a revival remedy and by the time the wedding was over she ended up with a group of wide-awake drunks. It was hours before any of them were able to drive home. The royal marriage lasted just a little longer.

One of the worst self-confessed spikers of drinks was 'Chips' Channon, the 'queen' of London society during the Thirties and Forties. He got his parties to go with a bang by adding Benzedrine to his cocktails. Another great man for cocktails was Jimmy, now no longer with us. Over the years he packed hundreds into his relatively modest house and served them the most atrocious sweet mixtures. At the last of these great parties, which, despite the cocktails, were enormous fun, he was asked where he had found the recipe. 'I heard it on the radio yesterday,' he replied, 'but I'm not sure if I wrote all the ingredients down.' To serve such deadly mixes one needs a lot of nerve and personality. There is a list of the more acceptable cocktails at the end of this chapter.

FOOD

Food at a drinks party is regarded as an option by some, and a necessity by others. Nuts and crisps suit some hosts perfectly well, particularly if the party is of a relatively short duration, or is a prelude to another festivity. If however guests are expected to down an amount of alcohol over a long period on empty stomachs, a certain amount of blotting paper in the form of food is required. The food can vary from caviar to egg sandwiches, to those popular little savouries (known as canapés in the U.S.), the ones that our family refer to as shaving cream on wet biscuits. Mini pizzas and quiches are always a great success, as are the old standby cocktail sausages, or bite-sized vols-au-vent.

Arrival

A warm welcome and a drink in the hand is the start of a good party, but firstly coats have to be left somewhere. A spare bedroom is usually assigned for this purpose, preferably one with its own bathroom. Hosts in a private house are not expected to lay on security, but it can be a problem. Some years ago, when fur was still worn, there was a spate of nasty incidents in the smarter postal code areas of Dublin. The owners of the latest and finest quality fur coats would find old-fashioned, mouldy-looking creations left in their place. When one light-fingered lady was tracked down she insisted it was a perfectly natural mistake. This exchange programme does not appear to be in operation with cloth coats, although raincoats can cause genuine confusion, with many a raincoat wearer losing not only their coat but the keys of the car.

When the guest has been supplied with a drink, it is time for introductions. At a small gathering this means going around the room but at a large party can be restricted to the immediate vicinity. An introduction with a tag is an invaluable ice breaker (see page 8). It gives complete strangers an instant starting point if they discover a common interest in sport, music, theatre, cooking, breeding pigs, organic farming, sky diving, skinny dipping, or multiple marriages.

Departures

'Have you no homes to go to?' many a host has muttered under his breath as what is termed the 'hard core' linger on, and on. It can be regarded as either a compliment to the quality of the party, or a damned nuisance, depending on the mood of the host. Just as irritating can be the jolly groups making plans for dinner later in the evening. They have descended like a swarm of locusts, drunk the host dry, left behind dirty glasses and overflowing ashtrays, and now, buoyed up by the hospitality received, are all set to carry on the evening's entertainment elsewhere.

From a guest's point of view nothing takes the joy out of a party like shutting down the bar. Half an hour is sufficient leeway to allow guests to linger. If the stated finishing hour is 8.30 the bar service could slow down then and cease at nine. Lights being switched on and off seems a bit much for a private function, though even that gesture is lost on many when they are tanked up and in full flow.

One wise couple always arranged to join their friends for a late dinner after their own party. At nine o'clock promptly they would put on their coats and bid farewell to the stragglers with the instructions, 'Do help yourselves,' with the rider 'and before you leave could you pop the glasses into the dishwasher'. Inevitably the 'hard core' beat them to the door. On a very serious note, it is always inadvisable to let anyone 'under the weather' drive home. In some countries the host is held responsible in law for the guest's condition.

Cocktail Party Characters

All cocktail parties have their fair share of characters. Of course they are present on other social occasions too, but alcohol and the easy accessibility to other guests, make them more apparent at drinks parties.

THE BORE

Bores are unavoidable: it is best to serve your time and then move on politely. Bores come into their own at the sticky start of a party and can be relied upon to break the ice without even noticing. Good friends can be rallied to ensure that newcomers are not pinned into corners.

It is a common fallacy that cocktail parties are the ideal way of offering hospitality to the uninvitable. If hosts have charitable instincts they should be indulged within the family circle — charity and drinks parties do not mix. Ann is a woman who does not suffer bores, either gladly or at all. If landed with one at a party, she will down her drink and look at them expectantly until the inevitable offer springs to their lips, 'Can I get you something?' 'Yes please,' is the equally inevitable reply, 'someone interesting to talk to'.

THE GROPER

After the initial unwanted contact this species is quite easy to avoid at drinks parties (dinner is another matter). The best method is to keep on the move and avoid the centre of the room, back to the wall providing the time-honoured protection. Non-smokers are at a disadvantage here, as nothing diminishes ardour like a short, sharp stab of a lighted cigarette.

THE TOO-TIMID-TO-MIX-GUEST

Truly shy people generally make an effort, it is the phonies that try the tongue-tied routine. Imagining that shyness or aloofness carries a social cachet, they stand to the side looking slightly lost while everyone else breaks their backs trying to include them. Ignore them. Sarah was an attractive, tough lady who played the shy card all her life. Women fussed around introducing her and asking their men to get her drinks and look after her. It was years before they discovered just how far their men had taken the 'looking after' instructions.

THE INSULTER

This species is closely related to, but more threatening in public than, The Begrudger. Begrudgers usually operate behind backs, Insulters preferring an up-front approach as, with alcoholically loosened tongue, they insist on telling fellow guests what they think of them. You can be assured that none of it is complimentary. On one occasion I overheard a well-known Insulter telling one of the country's leading writers, 'Not only are you a bore and a free loader, but you are a bloody awful writer to boot, and X thinks so too'. X in this case was the horrified host. Insulters always manage to make accomplices out of innocent bystanders. No matter how much a host attempts to assuage wounded feelings, the object of the insult will always hold him responsible too — after all The Insulter is his friend.

THE DRIVER

The Driver is not to be confused with The Bore, although the end result is much the same. The Bore can bore on any subject, The Driver is confined to what route he (always male) took to the party. Traffic congestion and how to avoid it is his only contribution to the conversation and it can be a useful one if one wishes to avoid a probable traffic build-up by travelling an extra twenty miles. The natural habitat for The Driver is London, however clones can be spotted in urban Ireland.

THE OVER–ACTIVE HOST

This species is mainly female. Far be it from me to criticise the party giver, however there are some hostesses who cannot bear to see two guests deep in conversation. As soon as two kindred spirits blend in conversation she destroys the intimacy by introducing a third person. Having wreaked havoc she then moves off to find new victims.

Popular Cocktails

ALEXANDER (aka Brandy Alexander)
⅓ Creme de Cacao, ⅓ fresh cream, ⅓ brandy. Shake on ice.

BETWEEN-THE-SHEETS
⅓ brandy, ⅓ Bacardi rum, ⅓ Cointreau, dash of lemon.
Shake on ice.

BLACK VELVET
Into a large glass simultaneously pour chilled Guinness and
iced champagne to taste.

BLOODY MARY
Essentially a mixture of ⅓ vodka to ⅔ tomato juice or V8 juice,
with a dash of Angostura Bitters (optional) and fresh lemon juice.
However, celery salt, vegetable juice instead of tomato, cayenne
pepper instead of Angostura, lime instead of lemon can all be used
according to individual taste. It can be shaken or stirred over ice,
and decorated with a stick of celery.

BUCK'S FIZZ
Chilled champagne and chilled fresh orange juice mixed
according to taste.

CHAMPAGNE COCKTAIL
The original recipe: put one lump of sugar in a champagne glass,
saturate with Angostura Bitters, fill with champagne and a slice of
orange. It is now customary to add brandy to taste.

CORPSE REVIVER
⅓ sweet Vermouth, ⅓ Applejack brandy, ⅓ brandy. Pour over ice,
stir, strain into glass.

DAIQUIRI
¾ Bacardi, ¼ fresh lime or lemon juice, dash of syrup.
Shake on ice.

EGG NOGG
Shake well and strain into a tumbler the following ingredients:
1 egg, 1 tablespoon sugar, 1 fl. oz brandy, 1 fl. oz rum.
Fill tumbler with milk, grate some nutmeg on top.

GIBSON
½ gin, ½ dry Vermouth, a pearl onion. Pour over ice, stir and
strain into glass.

HOT BUTTERED RUM
2 fl. ozs Jamaica rum, 1 sugar lump, 2 cloves, 1 fl. oz lemon juice,
small stick of cinnamon. Place all ingredients in tumbler, add hot
water and stir.

JOHN OR TOM COLLINS
Cracked ice, 2 fl. ozs lemon juice, 1 teaspoon caster sugar, 2 fl. ozs
gin. Fill with soda water, dash of Angostura Bitters, stir and serve
with slice of lemon. Brandy, rum or Whiskey Collins can be made
in the same way by adding each in place of gin.

KIR
Add a couple of drops of Cassis to a glass of dry white wine.
Kir Royale is made with champagne and Cassis.

MANHATTAN
⅔ rye whisky, ⅓ sweet Vermouth, dash of Angostura Bitters. Pour
over ice, stir, pour into glass, add cherry.

DRY MARTINI (original recipe)
½ dry gin, ½ dry Vermouth, pour over ice, stir, strain into glass.
Dry Martini (as currently drunk in the U.S.)
1 glass of gin, 1 or 2 drops of dry Vermouth, stir over ice, strain and
serve, adding a twist of lemon or olive as desired.

NEGRONI
⅓ dry gin, ⅓ sweet Vermouth, ½ Campari. Pour over ice,
add slice of orange.

OLD-FASHIONED

1 dash Angostura on a sugar cube, 2 fl. ozs rye or bourbon whiskey.
Pour over ice in a large glass, add slice of orange, a cherry and a
stirring rod.

PIMMS

1 measure of Pimms to 3 of lemonade or ginger ale. Pour over ice,
add mint and fruit, which can include orange slices and
strawberries. Serve in tall glass.

RUSTY NAIL

⅓ Drambuie, ⅔ Scotch whisky. Serve in large glasses over ice
with lemon twist.

SIDECAR

½ brandy, ¼ Cointreau, ¼ lemon juice. Pour over ice,
shake and serve.

STINGER

⅔ brandy, ⅓ white Crème de Menthe. Pour over ice, mix,
strain and serve.

WHITE LADY

½ gin, ¼ lemon juice, ¼ Cointreau. Pour over ice,
shake and serve.

The Weekend or House Party

'The first day a man is a guest, the second a burden, the third a pest.' (Edouard Laboulaye)

Hosting a house party is an expensive and time-consuming pastime, with guests to be looked after day and night for three days or more. On the positive side it is undoubtedly the most personal and most rewarding hospitality practised today. The perfect host invites a compatible mix of people and then creates a happy and welcoming atmosphere, one in which each guest will feel special, pampered and loved.

To ensure a smooth-running house party hosts should work out a check list well in advance complete with: bedroom allocation, menus and mealtimes, expected arrival and departure times, possible activities, as well as church services. One does not have to adhere strictly to such a list but it does provide a structure to work around (a deep freeze is essential for entertaining numbers over a period of time).

Making Guests Comfortable

When asked what he considered the most important attribute of a house party, Robert who is a young, rich and highly-sought-after house guest, summed it up in one word — warmth. Robert although susceptible to charm, is not the sort of young man to get carried away with being fussed over: the warmth he had in mind was of a more practical nature. He explained that lukewarm food was acceptable whereas a lukewarm bath was not. A nasty cold caught in a damp Kerry bedroom has taught him to take precautions in the form of an electric blanket. He travels nowhere without his 'comfort blanket' and an eclectic collection of plugs. He recounts that on many occasions the condensation rising from the damp beds he has slept in has reached Turkish bath proportions. After a warm and dry night's sleep he wakes up ready to tackle anything. Small wonder he is such a popular guest.

This story should alert all hosts to the importance of spending a night in their own guest room. Dipping beds and lumpy pillows would soon disappear, as would leaking shower faucets, jammed windows and half-hearted radiators. Mirrors and switches would be within reach of average-sized human beings. One medium-sized couple spent a weekend at a country house in County Meath without once catching a glimpse of themselves in the upstairs looking-glass. The mirror in question was placed over six feet high on the bathroom wall, so shaving and make-up had to be done by touch only. The puzzling thing was that both hosts were barely over five feet tall themselves.

It is a rare bedside light that actually works. The most common fault is that there is no bulb. Asking for a bulb within minutes of arriving does seem a little abrupt, so most guests leave the problem of the bulbless lamp for the next guest. The second problem is the socket. Experience shows that this is never located beneath the bedside table, but most commonly placed behind a double-doored mahogany wardrobe. If travelling without the aid of removal experts it is best to leave this problem also for the next guest to sort out.

BEDROOM NECESSITIES

Apart from an electric blanket and a working bedside light, a caring host will also provide an extra heater, or an open fire in rooms of gothic proportions. On a table will be a small tin of biscuits (in case the guest suffers from midnight hunger pangs), a carafe or bottle of water and a glass. Some hosts supply alcohol also but this is not expected. Some reading material could also be provided and it is always interesting to note by the books supplied how our tastes are perceived. The last time I stayed with friends in County Tipperary, *The Marquis de Sade*, *Growing Indoor Bulbs* and *International Jogger* were my lot. How the hosts came to such an odd selection is a mystery.

Towels (one decent-sized bath sheet), tissues, soaps, toothpaste, shampoo and bath essence should be laid out in the bathroom, but the first essential here is hot water.

Single beds are the safest bid in a spare room as they cover more contingencies than a double bed. Beds bring up the question of room sharing between unmarried couples. The more mature couples make their sleeping arrangements clear when accepting an invitation. Between young unmarried peers the decision is multilateral. Young couples staying with the older generation, particularly parents or elderly relatives, should accept what is offered, which is usually two separate rooms. What they do during the night is their own business. Hosts are entitled to run their own homes according to their own code of behaviour.

Organising Guests

To structure or not to structure their guests' stay always poses a problem as hosts do not wish to appear either sergeant majors or couch potatoes. The best house parties are carefully but unobtrusively managed. Whatever preparations are made must be flexible enough to allow for some deviation. Prepared plans should be voiced as suggestions rather than commands, for example, 'Some of us thought that a trip to the Antique Fair/Horse Show down the road might be fun' or 'Some hearties suggested a morning of mountain climbing, any takers?', rather than, 'Breakfast will be at 6.45 for tomorrow's mountain walk. Walking boots and rain gear are essential, no shirkers are allowed' — a nightmare scenario!

Meals

Mealtime structures should be explained. If a light breakfast is being served because a luncheon party is planned, that should be made clear beforehand, and not leave some poor guest who asked for a fry feeling like 'the boy who asked for more'. Likewise make it clear if the reverse is planned — a hearty breakfast followed by a light luncheon. Personal experience prompts me to urge guests to find out what the eating plans are for the day before turning down the offer of a substantial breakfast.

Let me share with you my eating pattern during a weekend in a County Wicklow mansion. We were due to arrive on Friday night in time for dinner. Previous weekenders had warned us to go easy on lunch as our hosts had a brilliant and generous cook. We were barely in the door when we were asked what we wanted for breakfast; a fry was mentioned to which my husband agreed enthusiastically. Confident that I was going to enjoy a wholesome dinner, I said 'Just a cup of coffee'. I should have mentioned there is but one food to which I am allergic and that is parsnips, but this had never posed a problem before. Dinner that night consisted of parsnip soup followed by roast pork covered with a creamy parsnip purée. I surreptitiously disguised my untouched meal and made plans to fall upon the pudding. At this moment our hostess announced that as the meal was so heavy we would just eat fruit. I ate most of it. Next morning while my husband trotted off to join the other trenchermen at breakfast I made do with my cup of coffee. As dinner was to be a heavy post-shooting party buffet at a nearby house, lunch consisted of smoked salmon sandwiches and Guinness. That evening everyone pronounced the main dish highly suitable for the occasion — pheasant and parsnip pie! Hunger forced me to leave before luncheon next day. I didn't dare ask what was on the menu!

Vegetarian or any other dietary requirements should be expressed in advance. Expecting to be catered for at the last minute is not only unreasonable, it is downright rude.

Clothes to Take

If there are plans for a sporting activity and a change into black tie for dinner every evening, it is only fair to issue a warning to guests. 'We will be changing for dinner' is sufficient notice for the initiated, but a newcomer to the house party code might need more specific instructions. 'Both evenings will be black tie' is more precise and indicates to the woman to bring two changes.

There is a Wodehouse story which deals, as do many of his stories, with the dress horrors of a country house weekend. A young man was bidden to join the rather grand family of his girlfriend at their country estate. Carefully packed in his inconspicuous brown suitcase were the suitable evening clothes. Dozing off on the train journey he almost missed his station, and in the ensuing rush he grabbed his case and jumped off. That evening when he went to his room to change, he found his clothes immaculately laid out — a clown costume. He had picked up the wrong case. The rest of the story is forgotten but he may well have strolled downstairs as a clown, looked around and said, 'Heavens I thought you said Fancy Dress!'

In general terms the dress code for country house weekends is: well cut, muted (must not frighten the horses), tweeds and cords, boots and walking shoes, vests, raincoats, warm cover-up dressing gowns and slippers (in case of a long walk to the bathroom), and of course evening clothes.

Tips

Tipping is expected. The larger the staff the easier the procedure. In very grand houses a lump sum can be given to the butler with instructions to apportion it as he sees fit. If you have used the extensive services of the maids for laundry or other assistance, it would be suitable to tip them separately. Some gourmands cannot be kept out of the kitchen where they insist on pressing money on the cook also. For some reason the chauffeur is rarely tipped, unless he has really gone out of his way for guests.

If in any doubt enquire from the host as to the going rate and to whom. They may mumble that it is not really necessary, but will, upon being pressed, be only too happy to suggest a suitable sum. There is an international servant network which puts out the word on non-tippers and certainly I have heard one couple disparaged over three continents.

Gifts for Hosts

When choosing a gift for the hosts, it should be kept in mind that chocolates, wine or flowers are not always suitable for the chatelaine of a fully staffed kitchen, fine cellar and elaborate gardens. Books are always a good standby, and will probably end up on your bedside table on the next visit, but do not write an inscription within unless requested. The idea of not writing an inscription is that the item can be recycled if desired. One elderly lady takes this notion to the limit and requests that her birthday and Christmas cards be unmarked also and a separate note inserted. She also re-uses her stamps and on being told it is illegal she insists, with some justification, that the Post Office is unlikely to jail an eighty-year-old.

Music in the form of a C.D. is another acceptable gift. Some original givers come up with croquet sets, complicated jigsaws or quite unique soaps and scented candles, the sort that are hand-made in a village just outside St Tropez. It is easier to give to hosts who do not have everything. A quality pâté or some other home-made delicacy is welcomed by anyone who has some extensive catering on their hands, so too is wine — here a case would be a suitable gift from a couple. If joining a house party where the expenses are being shared obviously none of this applies.

Guests — to Help or Not to Help

The greatest dilemma from the guest's point of view is whether to help, or keep out of the way. The very grand or the very simple establishments are easy to figure out. At the first, one is not expected to lift a finger, at the second, genuine, tactfully-proffered assistance is welcomed. It is the in-between that presents problems, the houses which boast some help, but not quite enough.

Experienced hosts will have planned their domestic routine so that all runs smoothly and appears effortless. The help they would most like from their guests is that they entertain each other. They might appreciate an occasional offer to fetch ice, pour drinks, carry a tray or fetch something or someone in the car. Chaotic hosts will be delighted with a potato peeler, washer up, children's entertainer and bar attendant. Frankly you would have been better off to stay at home.

STAYING OUT OF THE WAY

Staying out of the way is the tactful guest's passport to further invitations. The perfect guest has a finely tuned social antenna which tells them when to appear and when to become invisible. They can sense what the host really means when they ask, 'Would you like breakfast upstairs?' A helpful blunderer might row in with, 'Not at all, I love pottering about the kitchen in the morning'. Mr Tact knows instantly that his hosts would prefer the house to themselves in the morning. He has brought reading and writing material, probably even a pack of cards, enough certainly to keep him entertained and out of the way until he senses that the house is ready for him. An early morning walk can be indulged in as long as it does not bring the walker into contact with the domestic affairs of the household. Tidying one's own quarters is always acceptable and with the advent of the duvet, bedmaking is taken care of with one quick shake.

THE PERFECT GUEST

The perfect guest is the game guest — game for anything; one who is prepared to row in with enthusiasm with whatever plans the host may have, and one who is also capable of thinking for himself; one who does not expect to be entertained every moment of the day; one who does not sit like an expectant labrador with a lead in its mouth waiting for 'walkies'. A good guest can go 'walkies' on his own.

The perfect guests also know when to leave. They leave on time, immediately after Sunday lunch. If travelling by train, or other public transport, they enquire in advance as to what is the most suitable train, thus leaving the timetable in the host's hands. A noted weekend hostess, when questioned as to what she considered the most suitable time for departure said, 'Well before breakfast'. Guests should insist that they have to get on the road early she explained, and should leave as soon as they wake up. 'I lie in bed in the morning until I hear the last car depart, then I pad downstairs to a deliciously deserted house and do a jig in my empty kitchen.' One cannot expect friends to comply with this hostess's eccentric, but understandable request. All that one can hope is that guests do not drag out their departure.

The ever welcome guest is:

- Punctual
- Positive
- Healthy
- Pet and child free
- Suitably togged out
- Willing
- House-trained
- Helpful
- Discreet

The Grand House — What to Expect

Staying in well-staffed houses can put a strain on one's budget. It is not a question of tipping, it is the investment in presentable underwear. Bear in mind that when the cases disappear from the hall they have been taken upstairs to be unpacked. The contents will be taken out, laundered, brushed, and arranged in drawers and wardrobes. The question then is can your under-garments stand up to such scrutiny? As a teenager Alice spent a weekend in the grandest house in Cheshire, a castle actually. Together with some school friends she was invited for a 'coming out' dance. From the outside she looked like your average well-turned-out school leaver of the late Fifties, but underneath just about everything was held together with safety pins. Her well-worn ball dress consisted of yards of pale blue tulle, and looked romantic by candlelight but decidedly seedy in a bedroom as well-lit as an operating theatre. Laid out on the bed beside the dress was her clean but discoloured underwear and its non-matching safety pins. The palatial marble bathroom was desecrated by a pair of faded school pyjamas, complete with Cash's name tapes, and placed beside the basin were her squeezed-out tubes of Max Factor. Had she but known what to expect, all would have been pristine. You have been warned.

John's story is also a tale of the unexpected, or the unprepared. John is a musician, a man who lives in boiled shirts and tails during a concert tour. At the end of just such a tour he joined a house party in the Bahamas. On the evening he arrived there appeared to be more than the usual bustle in the laundry area. All became clear next day when he discovered that his 'laundry case' had been unpacked and the dozens of shirts therein had been washed, starched and ironed. Imagine his embarrassment when he realised the staff had worked late into the night on his behalf. He never intended to use his hosts' home as a laundry service.

The Thank-You Letter

Make no mistake, the thank-you letter is essential. You may have arrived laden with gifts, you may have been effusive in your gratitude on leaving, you may even have seen the host next day, nevertheless the thank-you letter is still considered necessary after staying in someone's house. Actually a thank-you letter is considered good manners following any hospitality. A cocktail party thank-you can be by telephone or in person. All thank-you letters should be written by hand.

The Dance

'Everyone knows that the real business of a ball is either to look out for a wife, to look after a wife, or to look after somebody else's wife.' (R.S. Surtees)

The dance, like the wedding, is a cause for a family gathering. In times gone by only those who could afford the expense, or the overdraft, gave big private dances. Quite apart from the how-much there was the where. Any large dwelling with its own ballroom, such as a castle, stately home or modern mansion is ideal.

These great private balls were given mainly for the offspring. In the case of the male it was to celebrate his 'coming of age' and traditionally this also gave the guests the opportunity to sample the Pipe of Port which had been laid down at his christening. The dance for the young woman was given when she reached the age of eighteen and was due to 'come out' in society. Weddings or other important anniversaries were also a reason for a ball. The hosts would fill their own house with guests and billet the overflow in the neighbouring grand houses: B&Bs fill the bill very well nowadays.

Now that everyone has got in on the act of hosting these lavish declarations of disposable income the scene has changed somewhat. Small houses expand with the addition of a tent, known as a marquee, in the garden, or if this is not possible the party is moved to an outside venue such as a hotel or a castle — a rented one.

Within a certain strata of international society, more noticeably in the U.K. or the U.S., 'coming out' dances are still *de rigueur*. They are frequently known as Debutante Balls. Their primary purpose in presenting young women into society is to introduce them to the marriage market. This is done by inviting all the eligible young men to the ball. These young men in their early twenties give the impression that the world owes them dinner, or at least free champagne, their only contribution being that they are single, male, and well turned out: they can be quite insufferable. However, as new breeds of escorts come on the scene each season and the invitations dry up, they soon return to normal. In today's career orientated world, by broadening the guest list these social occasions can also be utilised as an introduction to the job market. The more apparently democratic the world of commerce, the more important are connections.

Dance Invitations

The usual form is that the hostess sends out invitations to a large cast for the dance, but to a group, composed of family and close friends, for dinner beforehand. The rest of the invitees are farmed out for dinner to local hostesses. When the dance hostess has sorted out her list she will pass the selected names on to the dinner hostess who will contact her dinner guests.

Dinner Hostesses

It may appear a tremendous imposition to land ten or twenty unknown dinner guests on a neighbour, and indeed it is, the only consolation being that the neighbour's turn will come too. From the dinner party hostess's point of view, once she knows that the dance is planned she would be wise to volunteer her dining table. Conscription is definitely on the cards, willing volunteers always win Brownie Points, and she may even get to throw in a few of her own friends. If invitation is by card, it will be the usual card for dinner; on it she will announce 'For the O'Brien Dance' or 'Prior to the O'Brien Dance'. Dance hostesses can be tremendous bullies as to what time their farmed-out guests must arrive at the dance. If there is a grudge between the two hostesses it could surface here. Dinner hostesses have been known to detain their guests virtually until the last waltz.

Tim and Anne

Mrs Joseph Bloggs

at Home

Saturday 29th July

R.S.V.P.
15, Thornhill Road,
Dublin 2

Dinner — 8 o'clock
Prior to the O'Brien Dance

Catering
DINNER

As already mentioned some of the dinner catering for a large dance will have been taken care of by obliging neighbours. However the dance hostess still bears the brunt of it. Some parties, especially in this country, are entirely catered for by the hosts.

The dinner party guests are bidden to arrive at eight, drinks are served until about 9.15 when everyone goes into dinner. On these formal occasions the guests are seated with *placement*. Sometimes name cards are handed to guests as they arrive, giving them the number of their table which in turn can be checked off against a table plan, normally located near the dining area. A colour theme may also be employed, where the guests are given a colour which corresponds to their table.

Dinner may be served or semi-served. Often the first and last courses are served and the main course is buffet style. This is quite a good idea as it allows for a little mingling time in between. Three courses and coffee is usual for catering on this scale. At the end of the meal a cake might be wheeled in if it is an anniversary and the host may stand to say a few words. As he has paid for the entire evening it is only fair to listen with attention and to applaud with enthusiasm. At this stage the music starts and the hosts prepare to greet the next wave of guests.

BREAKFAST

Breakfast appears any time from 2 a.m. onwards. Eggs, bacon, sausages, and all the old favourites are still top of the bill, together with rolls, croissants, preserves, tea and coffee. A more elaborate breakfast can include kedgeree, kippers and even soup. The meal is buffet style and timing is elastic, ideally it should be available for a couple of hours. By this stage the dancers are ravenous and in need of something solid. Breakfast reunites the party by attracting back those stragglers who have lost their way in the grounds, and also acts as a watershed, dispersing the older revellers and bringing about a second wind in the young ones.

DRINKS

What drinks you serve depends on what you can afford. Champagne or cocktails made with it are a festive pre-dinner drink. Wine appears with dinner, and most hosts continue to serve wine for the rest of the evening, and, of course, plenty of water; beer is sometimes supplied after dinner. Vintage champagne can be drunk throughout the evening, but that is very costly, and it is preferable to supply a decent white wine rather than a cheap champagne, which can give appalling hangovers.

Music and Dancing

'Dancing is a perpendicular expression of a horizontal desire.'
(George Bernard Shaw)

Good music is central to a successful dance. Nowhere is the generation gap more apparent than in musical tastes, with a clear split between the two camps. If the budget extends to two bands, then start with the 'golden oldies', giving them their waltzes, foxtrots and above all their 'rock and roll'. When they have worn themselves out bring on the heavy metal. The same applies whether the music is live or recorded. Having two dance venues, one with regular lights and sound, the other with flashing lights and amplification is supposed to cater for both tastes at once, but regular dance-goers maintain it breaks up the party too much.

Hiring popular bands is an expensive proposition, but it can turn a good party into a memorable one. One evening that forever remains in the mind of the octogenarian jazz violinist, Stefan Grapelli, took place in the south of France many decades ago. He and his group of young, attractive musicians were engaged to play at a private dance, the fee offered being far in excess of their usual one. There was one condition however, that as party guests were going to be in the nude, they were required to play naked. Young, confident, and contemplating the fee, they agreed. On the night they were shown to their podium which was separated from the dancers by curtains. They were instructed that as they started to play the curtains would be drawn back, which they were, revealing two hundred fully-dressed dancers!

There are some dance steps which even the clumsiest should try to master. One is the waltz, another is the accommodating quick-step, accommodating because with a little imagination it can be adapted to just about any rhythm. South American dances are best left to those who know them, and men should remember that their hips do not gyrate with quite the same grace as do women's. If we saw ourselves dance many of us might be in for a rude shock as was Bob Hoskins: 'The choreographer convinced me that I looked like Fred Astaire, and I never doubted it. But when I saw the film...I thought I looked like a little hippopotamus shaking its hooves.'

Irish, Scottish and American set dances can be great ice-breakers and good fun, but a really stern bully is needed to marshal everyone into their places.

Subscription Dances

Private balls are few and far between, but fund-raising is always with us. Subscription or charity dances are a regular feature of the social calendar. There are Hunt Balls, College Balls, Club Dances and Charity Balls. There is no special etiquette attached to these occasions except to spend, spend, spend and above all to return the compliment. If friends support your charity, you must support theirs.

Gate-crashers

There is gate-crashing and gate-crashing. We are not dealing with the climb-over-the-wall and join-in-for-a-dance-variety here. No, we are talking here of people with the neck of a giraffe. These gate-crashers do not 'crash' on the night of the party, but solicit or demand invitations well in advance. Lady G. has nerves of steel and a determination to be at every event of importance. She heard that a certain tycoon was giving a big dance and when no invitation arrived she felt quite put out. Most people would say 'Well, there will be another time' or sulk and vow never to speak to him again. Not Lady G. She telephoned his secretary, said her invitation had not arrived and would they please send another one at once.

The lost invitation is a popular ploy. Some invitations are the means of entry to an event, bearing the legend 'please present this card'. This does not faze the would-be crashers, but spurs them on to greater heights of inventiveness. The method they employ is a polite acceptance to an invitation which they have not received, and an enclosed note which explains that as the invitation was mislaid could they please have another.

Of course not all these ploys work but most 'crashers' play percentages. They frequently use innocent accomplices to gain entry, either by arranging lifts, or meeting beforehand for a drink and arriving as one cosy group. Many a timid reader must wonder, are they not embarrassed when found out? Not a bit of it. Anyone who imposes themselves where they are not wanted has little sense of shame.

Children's Parties

'Punctuality is the politeness of Kings.' (Louis XVIII, 1755–1824)

Nowhere, but nowhere are polite kings more in demand than at a children's party. Parents who do not deliver their children on time maintain the young host's suspense at breaking point. An incomplete children's party is like Hamlet without the Prince. The party proper cannot start until the entire cast is assembled.

If dropping off the young party-goer calls for a tight time schedule it is nothing compared to what is demanded on the 'pick-up'. Woe betide the laid-back parent who arrives an hour late to find their little angel tearful and the hosts frantic. All children's parties should be organised with the same precision as a military campaign. The very young don't mind a tight structure being imposed, in fact they are happiest within known boundaries, but although teenage parties need an even tighter structure they must be perceived as being casual. The only way to achieve the desired 'chilled out' appearance is through organisation.

Toddlers

'The main purpose of children's parties is to remind you that there are children more awful than your own.' (Katharine Whitehorn)

Inviting toddlers means inviting their mothers or nannies also. Mothers are preferable as nannies tend to report back only the errors, mothers being too busy comparing their darlings with his or her peers to notice anything untoward.

The usual party time is in the afternoon between three and five. Two hours is pushing a toddler's attention span to the limit. When the guests arrive just putting them down within crawling or toddling distance of each other is enough to distract them. As toddlers are too young for even the most basic games, placing an array of toys around them should get the party going with a bang, often too much of a bang. When guests pick up the toys a possessive young host is likely to give them a wallop with whatever is at hand. This learning to share process is a long, slow, difficult one, even some adults are still learning.

Summer parties have an advantage over winter ones as a garden can yield dirt to smear and insects to examine as well as leaving an unsullied household. Planned parenthood means summer birthday parties.

Tea should arrive at the soonest possible moment. The adults need it and the children like to play with it. Carefully prepared delicacies for toddlers are as 'pearls before swine'. The junkier the menu, the more popular the food. Once fed, the attention span is exhausted and home is the next logical step.

Three to Five

There is no point in starting games or any form of entertainment for the three- to five-year-olds until all guests have arrived and handed over their gifts. The custom of exchanging presents is as old as time itself and nowhere is it more strictly adhered to than at children's parties. Guests arrive with a present and leave with one. Presents change hands whether it is Christmas, birthday or summer solstice. There is a school of etiquette which suggests that all gifts be handed over to the parents and opened later, the charming idea behind such a custom being to let the young host know that his guests are not just invited for what they bring. I have never seen this in practice, neither have I witnessed an eclipse of the moon.

Once all have handed over their 'ticket' to the party, the games begin. The idea behind games or entertainment is to tire out the participants in the shortest possible time. An active beginning means a relaxed finish. A couple of important facts to bear in mind are, the older the children the more space they need and boys need twice as much space as girls. One mother aptly described a boys' party as 'an afternoon of light fighting'.

Food at this age should be divided equally between sweet and savoury; taste buds are coming into their own and baby snacks are not appreciated. Once again there is no need to attempt a healthy, balanced meal but best to give a choice between such delicacies as mini pizzas, chips, chocolates, fizzy drinks and ice cream.

Five to Fifteen

These can be awkward years and parties need to be well structured with no time for boredom or introspection: straight into games, followed by tea and then a video or a hired entertainer. A common parental error is to imagine their guests less sophisticated than they are. Punch and Judy is an embarrassment for anyone over eight.

One of the most successful mixed age spreads was held in one father's sports club. Gift-bearing guests were greeted on the playing pitch, relieved of their presents and pinned with a coloured badge indicating their age suitability for the various races about to take place. Two or three large sport-playing friends of the father helped out, their bulk and enthusiasm freezing any protests. Races were run, whistles were blown, medals awarded, everyone won something. Tea arrived in individual bags — hamburgers, chips, crisps, wrapped chocolate biscuits, sweets and cans of soft drinks. Many a shy loner carried their meal to the edge of the pitch to enjoy the action at a safe distance. The group united for the traditional cutting of the cake and the out-of-tune rendering of 'Happy Birthday'. The major trophies were awarded and the young champions returned home exhausted.

'What if it rains?' is the constant concern in this country. The hearty organiser of this party had dismissed such sissy fears by pointing out that skin was waterproof, whereas his more realistic wife had made contingency plans for taking over the club ballroom.

The upper age limit within the five to fifteen age bracket prefer to be entertained and a theatre or cinema works very well followed by a meal out or at home. Adventure sports and picnics may be too much for budding couch potatoes. As children grow older their tastes in food become more sophisticated. A fairly safe guideline is — if it is expensive they will probably like it and smoked salmon and crab claws can prove as popular as pizzas and hamburgers.

Going Home Presents

We have already discussed the ritual handing over of gifts and the expected return. The arrival presents are dealt with by the guests' parents but the going home presents are the responsibility of the young host's parents. One can only hope they will prove responsible, unlike the highly original mother who liked to send her son's friends home with a gift they would remember: few have forgotten the goldfish in plastic bags or the rabbits in boxes. Young party leavers are happy with a balloon or a packet of sweets; slightly older children may enjoy a book or coloured pencils whereas the older guests are expected to have passed that stage.

Teenage Parties

Teenagers live in a private world, one that is closed to anyone outside their age group. The only way to entertain teenagers is to ask them what they want. But, and this is a big but, whatever the form of entertainment it must be carefully supervised. Parents can be a bit of a damper so perhaps a family retainer or in-between-aged friend can be pressed into service, preferably one with a black belt in judo.

A good example of what can go wrong was the party that Alice gave for her sixteen-year-old son. Because she found his friends obnoxious she decided to have a big drinks, eats and dancing party, seven to midnight — guilt drives women to madness.

The first inkling she had of trouble was when she heard the young host telling total strangers on the telephone, 'sure you can come and bring your friends'. Word was on the street. Gangs, not groups, turned up bearing brown paper bags which contained either vodka, which they drank neat, or bottles of beer which they opened with their teeth! The house was bursting at the seams, the music was thumping, teenagers were throwing up, couples had to be routed from bedrooms. Chaos reigned. The police were called when fights between rival gangs, all of them unknown to the host, broke out. An isolated incident? It can happen anywhere if the controls are not strict.

Food for teenagers has only one prerequisite — it must be identical to the food served at every other teenage party that season. Alcohol, if served, is best not interfered with, that is, no punch or 'cup' of any kind, just straight wine or beer.

The Art
of Saying Goodbye

I t is said that a man never knows how to say goodbye and a
woman never knows when to say it. A sweeping statement but
one with more than a grain of truth. Once the decision to
leave has been made — move. Hesitancy creates an aura of unease.
Brian and Ann love parties, they are good guests, they mix well and
contribute a great deal. Neither are they the last to leave, so what is
the problem? The problem lies in their inability to say goodbye.
They are ruthless in their thoughtlessness. A good hour before
departure the signals commence, first the questioning, slightly raised
eyebrows, answered with a nod. Those engaged in conversation
with either of them instantly wind down in preparation for their
immediate leave-taking, the hosts adjust their expression to that
mixture of regret and relief, and prepare their murmured 'Do you
really have to?' speech. Nothing happens. Another half hour may
pass before the next stage. This is the tapping of the watch and the
'Remember your early appointment', followed by copious
explanations as to why they have to leave early, although it is not
actually early at all.

Ann fetches her coat while Brian, now the centre of an uneasy
audience, bores with unwanted explanations. Instead of discreetly
waiting for Ann in the hall he keeps the party on edge. A well
wrapped Ann sweeps in and moves graciously around the room
bidding fond farewells and launching into at least two more conversations. At this stage the other guests, now thoroughly ill-at-ease,
start to move also. The long goodbye has discomfited everyone and

there is no murmured 'Do you have to?' from the hosts who are now contemplating hurling the couple through the closed windows.

Having successfully broken up the party, Brian and Ann now proceed to give their hosts frostbite and send their heating bills rocketing, with a litany of what a good time they had and extended effusive thank-yous at the open door. They are a particular menace in the city as the goodbyes are repeated once again from their car, which could be parked half a block away. By now the neighbours are awake and the final toot-toot on the horn rouses the rest of the road.

The perfect guest leaves quickly and quietly

As everyone is under different time pressures — far too boring a subject for conversation — it stands to reason that some leave before others. Best not to make an exhibition of one's self, as the matron in my boarding school used to warn attention grabbers. Best to stand up, after a discreet signal to one's partner — some partners refuse to acknowledge signals, such behaviour does not fall into the etiquette category, more the Training of Loved Ones, a subject on which nobody has as yet written the definitive guide — say a quick goodbye and leave quietly. The hosts can then relax with the remainder of the guests, or what is often known as 'the hard core'.

In the case of large gatherings if the host is not in sight it is acceptable to slip away without expressing one's gratitude, provided that this is done next day. In the case of long liquid parties, going in search of hosts or anyone else is to be discouraged. Discretion accepts that a coat may be removed from a bed as long as the occupants remain undisturbed. Neither is leave-taking the time to make complicated social arrangements or business deals as at this point of the evening the hosts are usually on automatic pilot. Always aim to leave your hosts regretting your departure.

A car-less woman should be wary of accepting lifts as she could leave herself open to all manner of proposition. Take the case of Ann and a young friend of her son. Her husband was away, she took a taxi to the party and accepted a lift home from the 'boy'. On the way home they passed his flat, which he pointed out, saying without thinking — 'I'd ask you up for a cup of coffee, but I haven't changed the sheets'!

Finally, once departed, never return. If an item, other than the car keys, has been left behind, let it stay there until next day unless you want to experience what Gwladys did in County Meath. Gwladys was very much a city woman, a friend of politicians, writers and the media. On a whim she accepted an invitation from members of the horsey set. The evening dragged. At the earliest acceptable moment Gwladys and her friends made their departure. While still in the driveway she discovered that she had left her gloves behind. They drove back to the house, she ran in through the unlocked door to find the remaining guests dancing around the hall chanting 'They've gone, at last they've gone'!

Table Manners

'**B**ad table manners, my dear Gigi, have broken up more households than infidelity.' (from *Gigi* by Alan Jay Lerner)

Good table manners are basically a combination of common sense and sensitivity. The knife is not put in the mouth because it could cause a nasty injury. The mouth is not kept open when eating because mastication is not a pretty sight. Speaking with a full mouth can distribute the contents, an even less attractive sight. Cutting food with elbows akimbo means a dig in the ribs for neighbours. Expansive gestures with knife and fork in hand, can lead to serious injuries. A man lost his eye like that, the culprit his sister, but as she had just been disinherited in his favour, it may not have been an accident. Then there are the frills which are derided as etiquette, they too started with common sense, but some of them ended up downright pretentious.

Not knowing how to eat a particular food or what to do with implements is no disgrace. Always bear in mind that other people (never oneself) enjoy feeling superior. They will love to be consulted. Watch them preen as you ask 'How do I tackle this artichoke?', or 'Which fork is correct for the prawns?' Go ahead, make their day, act dumb.

Anyone who is happy with their table manners can ignore the following rules and regulations laid down and embellished over the years. But if in doubt it might be worth checking. Good table manners resemble a Masonic handshake, they signal, without words, whether or not you are a member of the club. The club in this instance is made up of those who were taught, or picked up, the customs of polite society at table.

Children's Manners

Table manners, unlike the best bib and tucker, should not be kept for show. Constant practice makes perfect, and children should learn by example; natural mimics that they are they will pick them up. They in turn will be well-mannered little ambassadors for the family. Good table manners are as essential as toilet training, slobs are not endearing. Constant exposure to correct table manners will wear down even the toughest rebel. As well as being mimics children are also broadcasters. Many a household has set the table with extra little refinements only to hear the young observer announce to the guest, 'We don't usually have napkins, only when we have visitors', or 'What is that little knife doing in the butter?'

Conversation at Table

'Good manners is the art of making those people easy with whom we converse. Whoever makes the fewest persons uneasy is the best bred company.' (Jonathan Swift)

Nobody, least of all this retiring author, would dream of suggesting what to talk about at table. The question is, who to talk to?

Table placing gives every guest two dinner companions and well-mannered diners will remember this and divide their attention accordingly. It is customary to turn with the courses, a bit like the road safety code, look right, left, and right again. Each course indicates a natural division of time. By the pudding a little leeway is permitted, and the guest of your choice gets more attention, always taking care that neither neighbour is left unattended for long. A shared meal is a team game.

Shy guests, who are unable to push themselves, will be looked after by this gentle rule. Unfortunately, there are people who do not follow the rules and they monopolise one neighbour and unbalance the rest of the table. Hopefully the light will dawn for them some day, in the meantime their more socially aware companion can say, 'I mustn't monopolise you any more' and turn to the guest at their other side.

The worst offenders in the every-talker-has-two-sides game, are the social climbers. When they discover that, in their estimation, they have struck gold on one side and dross on the other, they condemn themselves by their own actions. Some diners may find the company at the far side of their immediate neighbour more interesting so they talk across them. Banishment is too kind a fate for such selective bad manners. Caroline, an attractive widow, was seated beside a barrister called Kevin. On her other side was a judge. Throughout the meal Kevin treated her as the invisible woman in his efforts to impress the judge. Caroline never forgot. Her long memory was of little service to Kevin when she and the judge were married. The moral here is if good manners do not influence you, try self-preservation.

The old rules of table conversation were: steer clear of politics, religion and sex, and never mention the food. How times have changed! Without politics, religion and sex a great silence would descend on the Irish table. However the suitability of the company should be borne in mind. Whereas politics in a general sense is acceptable, getting personal can lead to trouble and conversation should be halted before blows are exchanged. Religion might be a controversial subject in some parts of the island, and sex, if names are mentioned, can lead to no end of complications, let alone law suits. This writer was present at a dinner where one of the guests decided to recount the latest 'sex and politics' scandal. Brian, not normally a gossip, launched into an account of what the first citizen had said to a government minister regarding his blatant womanising, and particularly concerning his latest conquest. The tale was mild compared with some and inoffensive to the point of blandness, except to the mother of the latest conquest who was sitting beside the storyteller. What is the etiquette in dealing with a situation like that? Frankly there is none, other than to change the subject and carry on the conversation. When the shock has died down a quiet apology would be in order.

Setting the Table

Tradition has a lot to recommend it when it comes to tables, and table settings. Glass-topped tables can look amazing when lit from underneath, but they can be unnerving to sit at. Legs are on display. There is no opportunity to kick off your shoes, or make affectionate gestures below table, even a run in a stocking is spotlit for all to see. Marble is fine in warmer climates but can be both cold and hazardous. Anything laid down on it with emphasis is sure to splinter. A traditional wooden table is safest.

A tablecloth should be used for dinner — mats are acceptable but more suitable for luncheon. In an emergency a well-starched sheet can double as a cloth for a large table. Next come cutlery, glasses, table napkins, condiments, butter dishes with knives, and decoration. Common sense dictates that flowers and candles are kept below eye level, unless employed as a screen to keep warring factions apart (this has been known to happen with family parties).

CUTLERY

All eating implements are placed on the table in such a way as to enable the diners to work their way from the outside in (see opposite). For a meal consisting of soup, fish, meat and pudding, the setting is soup spoon on the outside right-hand side, beside it a fish knife whereas the fish fork is the first in line on the fork side. One step in come the meat knife and fork.

The pudding spoon and fork could round it off on the inside, or they could be placed across the top of the place setting

A formal dinner table setting

(see Pudding Spoons and Forks, page 87). The bread knife, which is smaller than the meat knife, could be placed on the bread plate or to the right of the knives, or even across the top with the pudding implements. If a dish arrives at table boasting its own implements, use them. Restaurants are less confusing in that they employ the supply and demand method, when the dish arrives so too does the appropriate cutlery.

There is more to table manners than holding a knife and fork in the 'correct' way, but it appears to be one of the major dividing lines between the know-it-alls and the dumb-as-dammits.

First rule — do not hold them as pencils. The handles of both are buried firmly in the palm of the hand, the index fingers placed where the blade meets the handle on the knife, and in approximately the equivalent place on the fork, with the tines pointed downward. The tips of the handles should not be on view. Ah, you say, how about American customs? Table manners and American eating habits can be mutually exclusive. U.S. books on etiquette indicate a preference for European table manners as they are neater, faster, quieter, and both more attractive and more practical.

FORKS

So when does the fork go solo? Quite simple really — when food does not need cutting, as in the case of lasagne or other pastas, quiches, other soft foods, or bite-sized pieces. When using the fork alone the tines should be pointed upwards. Eating peas with a fork may yet become part of the Olympic decathalon event. Let's face it they are impossible to eat in the accepted way, which is pressed very gently to the back of the fork. Reversing the fork is frowned upon but is common practice, and common sense, say I. Puddings such as soft cakes and tarts may also be eaten with a fork alone. Fish is a soft food but a knife is required to separate the bones from the flesh.

FISH KNIVES AND FORKS

Special implements for fish are a relatively recent addition to culinary confusion. Fish forks look like forks whereas fish knives are flat, blunt instruments. A sharp knife is not effective in removing fish from the bone, but two forks are. If you do not possess fish knives, do not give it a thought, you can always play 'old-fashioned' and use the two fork trick to confound snobs.

SOUP SPOONS

The soup spoon is another modern innovation at table. Prior to the rounded, deep-bowled spoons, a large spoon or serving spoon was used. It has to be said that soup spoons are handier to manage. The correct spoon manoeuvre is to hold the spoon parallel to the body, scooping up the soup by moving the spoon outwards. As the liquid recedes in the dish, the dish can be tilted, also away from the body, (see Soup, page 92).

KNIVES

There is little to be said about knives, except that they are used for cutting only, not for scooping, gesticulating or pointing.

PUDDING SPOONS AND FORKS

Pudding spoons and forks are last to be used if cheese is being served French-style, that is, before pudding, second-last if cheese is being served English-style or after the pudding.

The pudding spoon and fork are sometimes placed across the top of the place setting, the fork with its base to the dinner fork (on the left) and the spoon above with its base toward the dinner knife. That is the position in which they should be picked up, the spoon in the right hand and the fork in the left. Left-handed people will have worked out their own method by now. These little instruments should be used together. If the pudding is ice cream or soufflé the fork can be ignored, and the spoon likewise for tart or cake.

SMALL SPOONS

Small spoons appear at the oddest moments. In the United States one cannot get through a meal without at least a passing acquaintance with them. There they serve fish, such as prawn cocktail, in glasses with a teaspoon on the side. I think plates are preferable.

Then again they rear their little heads for ice cream or a similar concoction, even growing long handles in the process. Slightly smaller are the demi-tasse spoons which accompany small coffee cups. Further down the scale are the tiny spoons set beside mustard dishes and salt cellars. Some French restaurants lay a reversed flat spoon beside the entrée plate — this is for sauce. Do not let it confuse you: ignore it, bread is better to mop up sauce.

TRICKY IMPLEMENTS

Following the host's lead is the only safe bet when dealing with the unknown. Mind you, blind adherence can have its pitfalls too as afternoon tea guests at the White House discovered. The President in office poured his tea into his saucer, the company followed suit, but realised their error when he placed the saucer on the floor for his dog!

Snail Tongs

Snails arrive in a deep dish — to hold the garlicky butter — and beside them are laid a pincers and a long-pronged fork. The pincers are held in the left hand, and used to grip the shell, leaving the opening uppermost. Then the fork is used to spear the snail and remove it from the shell. It is the same principle as periwinkles and pins — only posher.

Asparagus Holders

The incredibly pretentious serve their hot asparagus with a special tongs or holder. Untouched by human hand the spears are picked up, dipped in butter and conveyed upwards to the mouth. Fingers feel much more satisfactory.

Pickle Fork

A pickle fork is for fishing pickles out of a deep dish or jar and has two long thin prongs. If you have not got one, don't lose any sleep.

Cheese Knife

A cheese knife has a curve at the end of the blade which culminates in two sharp prongs, the idea being that you cut the cheese and then spear it on to your plate.

Nut or Lobster Cracker

As the name suggests the nutcracker is for opening nut shells, but is also used for cracking the claws of shellfish. In the writer's opinion this messy job should be dealt with in the kitchen and the diner required to do no more than pick daintily at their food, while engaged in fascinating conversation. However life is not always as it should be and far too frequently food arrives at the table in a semi-edible state. So it is that sometimes crab, crayfish and lobster claws arrive complete with D.I.Y. nutcracker and a skewer. How to cope?

The shell is picked up in the left hand and the nutcracker used to crack it firmly in a couple of places so that meat can be extracted with the point of the skewer. This can be a messy operation as shells, if fresh, contain liquid which squirts out once cracked. As for the fingers, a ewer and basin rather than a finger bowl are called for.

See why I prefer to leave these preparations to those who are paid to do them?

Small bone or plastic spoons

Small bone spoons — plastic only if desperate — are used for caviar. Aficionados declare that metal taints the eggs slightly.

Tricky Foods

'No one can make you feel inferior without your consent.' (Eleanor Roosevelt)

Certain foods are described as 'an acquired taste'; usually they are rare and expensive and acquiring the taste could lead to insolvency. Sometimes these foods also require acquired eating techniques. Let us examine the story of M. and the gulls' eggs. M.'s initiation to this delicacy came about at a smart young party in London. Teenage M. was served a half-dozen mini speckled eggs on a plate; being a bit shortsighted and heavily engaged in chatting up the chap beside her, she gave only cursory attention to the eating methods employed by the other diners. They seemed to pop them in their mouths whole. M. followed suit, shell and all. Her companion, no longer deceived by her pseudo-sophisticated line in chat, attempted to point out her error. M., a stubborn girl, would not admit ignorance. 'The shell's the best part' she insisted. She chewed her way through all six eggs, and spent the rest of the evening removing particles.

This little story indicates that ignorance of a new food is no big deal, but not having the wit to observe carefully how the guests are dealing with it, is.

Lemon wedges arrive with most fish, and some other dishes. The idea is to squeeze them over the food, which can be done by spearing them with a fork or by using fingers only. This is trickier than it sounds, the secret being to get the acid juice on to the plate and not into the eye of your neighbour.

Mussels in dishes such as Moules Marinières arrive in their shells. The half shell is more correct but more labour intensive for the kitchen — again a case of the cook making the diners work. The shell is picked up in the left hand and the mussel forked out with the right hand. A more rustic approach is to use the discarded shell as a scooper, even more basic is eating directly from the shell, this however is very messy. A dish is provided for discarded shells, and a finger bowl for clearing up operations. When the fish in the shell is finished the soup can be eaten with a spoon, taking care to avoid occasional pieces of grit at the bottom.

Gulls' eggs are cracked on the side of the plate, shelled, dipped in salt and eaten.

Corn-on-the-Cob is really too messy a food to serve on a formal occasion. The skewers at either end serve as handles, the corn is rolled in the melted butter, picked up and eaten. The result is butter from ear to ear. In place of skewers, fingers can be used, the result then being butter all over the face and hands.

Avocado pear is served cut in half lengthways, accompanied by French dressing and eaten with a small spoon.

Artichokes present quite a challenge for the uninitiated. Globe artichokes look like small prickly cabbages. They can be eaten hot with melted butter or cold with vinaigrette. The technique is to pull out the leaves, dip them in butter or dressing and eat the tender bit at the base of each leaf. As the leaves get smaller they become more tender and yield up no more than a thin film of flesh. On reaching the centre, cut away the thistle-like covering over the heart, and eat with a knife and fork. Jerusalem artichokes are entirely different, looking like small gnarled potatoes, and are eaten boiled and in a purée or sauce. They create no problem in eating, but are said to cause wind.

Cheese should present no problems, but it does. Thoughtless eaters cut away the centre piece, leaving the drier edges for others. It should be cut in wedges, as one would a cake. With hard cheese the rind is cut off before eating, as this is its protective wrapping. Soft cheese is already wrapped in protective covering so its rind can be eaten. Stilton can be taken with a scoop or spoon.

Oysters are served raw in their half shells, and wedges of lemon, red pepper or tabasco may be served with them. Firstly, the fish is sprinkled with lemon, then the shell is picked up in the left hand and the flesh forked out with the right hand, and eaten and the juice is then drunk from the shell.

Prawns are best when served at table without their shells. Some large imported prawns are served grilled, shell and all. Again, simple for the kitchen, hard for the eater. The shell is removed by first getting rid of the head, and the little leg-like feelers, then the shell is cracked lengthways with the fingers and the fish eased out.

Spaghetti is not a dish to choose when wearing clothes labelled 'Dry Clean Only'. It is said that the sprinkling of Parmesan makes the strands grittier and easier to pick up. That may be so but the problem of the elusive dangling strands remains. Forks alone are used for pasta. The ribbons are coiled around the tines, and a spoon is sometimes employed in the left hand to act as a platform from which to twirl the pasta around the fork. A casual approach is the only one to adopt with spaghetti.

Whitebait are tiny, tiny fish served fried, complete with heads and tails and eaten whole with a squeeze of lemon juice. Travellers to the Far East assure me that grasshoppers are eaten in the same way.

Asparagus, as previously mentioned, can be eaten with a tongs, although fingers are more commonly employed. The vegetable is picked up by the thick end (it may bend a little), and the point rolled in butter or sauce before eating. Repeat with each mouthful. When the going gets tough abandon the stalk and move on to the next one, leaving the stalks at the side of the plate. With tinned asparagus the entire spear is eaten.

Pâté is served in a slice or mould on the plate, or passed around in a dish from which a wedge may be removed. It is accompanied by hot toast and a knife, the pâté being spread on the toast, bite by bite. Heaven, according to the Rev. Sydney Smith is 'eating pâté de foie gras to the sound of trumpets'.

Soup is one of the simplest foods to eat so why include it here? Because of the noise factor. There are those who ease the liquid gently into the mouth and those who employ the suction method. The hoover-type method is not to be recommended. It is said that at a dinner dance the waiter was dispatched to a noisy diner, requesting him to hurry up as 'the band was waiting to play'!

Glasses at Table

People let wine glasses get them into a tizz in just the same way as cutlery. There is no need. Any type of glass that holds liquid will satisfy thirsty guests. Toothmugs however, with their residue of toothpaste, are best left in student dorms.

For the purpose of drinking, the minimum requirement is a glass; if it is for wine then one with a shank looks best. Getting busier we add a water glass, this can be a tumbler, or a large-sized shank glass. Moving up the scale, there may be a choice of red or white wine, calling for two wine glasses. The glasses, whatever the number, are placed to the right of the place setting. Ideally they can be placed in order of use with the final glasses furthest away. However it is no great social sin just to clump them together. Usually the glass for the red wine is wider. A wider glass enables the wine to 'breathe' and the drinker to appreciate the 'nose'. The narrower glass keeps the white wine cooler. Entertaining on a grand scale means additional glasses. If sherry is served with the consommé it comes in a slightly smaller glass than the white wine, and if dry, it should be chilled. Also chilled is the white wine that follows with the fish (or some other suitable starter or second course). Red wine is served with the meat or game.

The glasses used during the rest of the meal could veer between white wine glasses once again for a sweet pudding wine, or champagne in narrow flute or tulip glasses. Wide champagne glasses have gone out of fashion; it is claimed that the narrower glass retains bubbles. Sometimes champagne is reserved for the toast.

After Dinner Drinks

Port, brandy or liqueurs are traditional after dinner drinks, although personal choice can run to more red wine or perhaps a whiskey. The wise, or drivers, might prefer to move on to water at this stage. Port is served in glasses slightly smaller than white wine glasses and it, or red wine, are excellent with cheese. Port is served at the end of a meal when the ladies have retired, if ladies withdrawing is on the agenda. The port is passed in a decanter, always to the left. It is therefore unhelpful to try and short-circuit the passage of the port by passing it to the right: no matter how long the delay in waiting for it to pass around the table, it should never move to the right.

Brandy is also offered at this stage, and is served in large balloon-shaped glasses. The cup or bulb of the glass sits comfortably in the palm of the hand, the fingers divide to slip in the stem. This enables the brandy to warm and release its aroma, often the fumes alone being sufficient to knock non-drinkers sideways.

Liqueurs may be offered at the dinner table. If the ladies move to the drawing room they are served there with coffee. Liqueur glasses are minute thimble-sized glasses on a stem — probably the most unsatisfactory glasses ever invented. Clearly, drinking liqueurs is not meant to be a comfortable, relaxing process.

Glasses without stems are tumblers and they come in all sizes. The largest size is used for beer, or long mixed drinks with ice. The next size down is good with most mixed drinks or spirits on the rocks. There are also large capacity stem glasses which can be used as tumblers.

Cocktail glasses were originally quite small, about the size of a sherry glass with a wide brim. As drinkers' capacities increased so too did the size of the glass. Some dry martini glasses in the U.S. are big enough to bathe a small baby in. Silver cocktail glasses, which once came in a set with silver cocktail shakers, have gone the way of domestic servants.

Cutglass or plain depends on taste. The very nature of cutglass means that its prisms reflect the light, making it an attractive and romantic addition to any table, it also follows that the glass is quite thick. Wine buffs prefer thin crystal, claiming they can 'feel' the wine through it. Silver wine goblets have major disadvantages; they can give the wine a metallic taste, there is no question of 'feeling' the wine through them, and a host has to stand up to see when a refill is necessary. Being more decorative than practical they make charming flower or candle holders.

Wine

There is a lot of nonsense and snobbery attached to wine. Do not let it intimidate. Buy what you like best within your means. No matter what the quality of the wine, the glass is never filled more than two-thirds full. If you find this custom stingy, buy bigger glasses.

White wine and dry sherry are served chilled, but there is no need for them to be so cold as to paralyse the taste buds as is the American fashion. Vodka can be knocked back iced, but that is a different matter altogether, and best left to the Russians.

Opening red wine in advance and keeping it at room temperature can improve the wine while some older wines with a heavy sediment need to be decanted. It is said that both expensive and cheap wines are better decanted as a mark of respect for the older wine and a mark of discretion with the plonk. Wine bluffers transfer their cheap wine into elegant decanters and bury the bottles — it's called making a silk purse out of a sow's ear!

An extensive knowledge of wine is a gift bestowed on those who study the subject, are blessed with an excellent memory and a large income. Enthusiastic wine buffs or 'grapies' have to curb a tendency to go on a bit about wine. If drinking with such a person it is wise to memorise a few phrases and adjectives used to describe wine: mellifluous, blackcurranty, gentle, harsh, young, old, flinty, smooth, big-bodied, thin, amusing, presumptuous, liquid grace.

No matter how rarified the palate, it is a mark of condescension to guests to serve them an inferior wine to what the host drinks.

Being an acknowledged wine expert or Master of Wine is not unlike bearing the title of 'Fastest Gun in the West', where expertise is constantly challenged. So it was with Tom, he of the finest palate in Ireland. One day in the middle of a blind champagne tasting he was called away to the telephone. While he was out of the room someone added flat beer to his glass. On his return he took a sip, and said in disgust, 'This tastes like piss'. His tormentors asked, 'But whose Tom?'

Spritzer — white wine with sparkling water — is the one drink that really irritates any self-respecting 'grapie', who would endorse this little couplet by G.K. Chesterton: 'And Noah he often said to his wife when he sat down to dine, "I don't care where the water goes if it doesn't get into the wine".'

Toasts

Champagne is the festive drink for toasts. When the champagne glass is filled at the end of a formal meal, it should not be drunk immediately as it usually signifies that a speech and toast are to follow. It is a cause of no little embarrassment to sit or stand for the toast with an empty glass. Following the defeat of the House of Stuart at the Battle of Culloden, staunch Jacobites always held their glasses over the water when requested to join in a 'Toast to the King', thus toasting their own monarch over the water while still keeping up appearances and holding on to their heads. As one is unlikely today to meet staunch adherents to the House of Stuart, this little anecdote has nothing whatsoever to do with modern table manners but is an example of how to do your own thing and still appear to conform.

The Toastmaster is the person who calls for silence for the speeches. The usual form is that the guest of honour is toasted and then he or she may reply. Then when the speeches and toasts are over, the toastmaster announces, 'Ladies and Gentlemen you may now smoke'.

In the case of a State dinner hosted by the President, let us say, for the King of Sweden, the toastmaster would announce the President. She would then make a formal speech emphasising the bonds between the two countries and ask the assembled company to rise for a toast to His Majesty the King of Sweden. The King would then reverse the procedure, make his speech and finish by asking the company to rise to toast Her Excellency the President of Ireland. State occasions may not be your lot, but the principle for the speeches and toasts is the same at even the most informal meal.

Mopping Up and Dunking

Mopping up sauces and gravies with bread is frowned upon at formal dinners such as State occasions. Considering that large catered functions rarely offer a sauce worth mopping up, this point of etiquette should not arise. Coming down the formality scale, it is considered acceptable to break a small piece of (unbuttered) bread onto the plate and give it a swirl with a right-handed fork. Personally I find it easier and equally inoffensive to do the same with a dainty morsel of bread held with the fingers of the right hand. What a fuss for a bit of sauce — it had better be worth it!

Opinions divide as to when dunking is permissible. Some say only when eating alone, others generously broaden the number to include the family.

Table Napkins

Table napkins are sometimes referred to as serviettes. Now here is a word that can divide company more completely than the Great Wall of China. Despite the fact that members of polite society major in pretentiousness and pepper their conversation with French words and phrases, the one word that never passes their lips is 'serviette'. Table napkin is what the white square of linen is called. This can be shortened to napkin, reluctantly. It can even be coloured — at a pinch it may be made of paper, but it is never a serviette.

The table napkin is placed, either directly in front of, or to the left of the diner. It can be laid down quietly folded, or more flamboyantly sculpted into the shape of a bishop's mitre, a swan, or whatever the imagination suggests. At the start of the meal it is shaken out and placed on the lap: it is not tied or tucked around the neck no matter how practical this may seem. During the meal it is used to wipe the fingers and dab at the mouth, to ensure that no spare crumbs or drops decorate the face.

When leaving the table, leave the napkin unfolded back on the table, except in some private houses where napkin rings are provided for each person — practical if slightly genteel. There is a story told of an elderly English Duke opening a village fête. While he wandered around the stalls his eye was caught by the gay little rings. 'What on earth are they for?' he enquired. 'They are napkin rings' His Grace was informed. 'They are used to fold table napkins for use again.' 'Good God, what poverty,' he stuttered 'do people actually use napkins a second time?'

Some Do's and Don'ts

◆ Do not loll on the chair or use the table as a prop.

◆ Elbows are just about acceptable on the table these days, but at the end of the meal, when you are engaged in conversation.

◆ Hands should rest on the table. The perceived correct position is to place the inside of the wrist lightly on the edge of the table. There was a strict English school of ram-rod straight backs and hands on the lap but continentals find this placing of hands unacceptable. They are intrigued as to what is going on out of sight. In days gone by placing hands on the table, in full view of the company, was an assurance that the guest was not fondling a dagger or a sword or, nowadays, a dining companion.

◆ Try not to fiddle, resist joining the label removers, flower de-headers, candle wax moulders, napkin pleaters, and cutlery movers.

- Do not lower yourself to meet oncoming food, bring it up to your level.
- Do not splay elbows. A dig in the ribs holds few attractions.
- Do not stretch. The perfectly mannered companion sees that you never have to do so by placing everything within reach. If you do the same it means you are helping yourself at one remove.
- When helping yourself to food, make a quick calculation as to the allotment. Leave the serving spoons side by side in readiness for the next person. If passing a dish around the table, hold it for the person beside you, they will extend the same courtesy to you. Politeness pays.
- Salt and pepper. Pepper is sprinkled from containers. Salt is placed with a salt spoon on the side of the dish, and used from there. Grinders for salt and pepper sprinkle only.
- Beware starting to eat before grace at a formal meal. Wait for a lead.
- Do not start to eat before all the accompaniments, such as vegetables and sauces, have been served. Neither is it polite to start until everyone has been served. Many a host insists that guests start but it is more polite to wait until they are ready. Also, if you wait for the hosts to lead the way there will be no confusion over what cutlery to use.
- Accidents happen. When they do, the only recourse one has is to apologise sincerely and offer to clean up or replace a damaged item, an offer which is usually refused. Some hosts might suggest sprinkling salt or soda water on spilt red wine, or slipping a napkin between table and wet cloth. Both hosts and guest should endeavour not to make a major production out of a mishap.
- Try not to mush up food, an irresistible temptation for eaters of berries and cream, or potatoes and gravy.
- It is important to know what to do with cutlery during the meal. When taking a break from eating, leave the knife and fork at an angle on the plate. This indicates to the waiter that you will resume at your leisure. When finished, the knife and fork are

placed side by side on the plate. This is a clear and well-established custom, but one of which some waiters are evidently ignorant, so at large functions it is a wise precaution to keep one hand on the plate when not actually eating, otherwise it will be whipped away. Waiters sometimes give the impression of being paid per plate removed, with a time fault penalty incurred if they delay.

♦ Eating with fingers should be indulged in only at picnics, not at the table. If the hosts proceed to pick their bones clean with their fingers one doesn't have to follow suit. The only exception to this rule is in countries where fingers only are used for food; there people do it with a deftness and delicacy that puts us implement-wielders to shame.

♦ Finger bowls appear at the side of the plate during a meal if the food is messy. Dip, rinse, and dry. If they land in front of you at the end of a meal, standing on a little mat, they are intended to be used with fruit or pudding. Pick up the bowl and mat and place them in front of your plate, leaving the plate itself clear for whatever is about to be served. Some hosts supply hot towels — a nice touch provided they are removed immediately, otherwise the table starts to resemble the bathroom of a seaside boarding house.

♦ There are some odd rules about eating bread at table. Although you may have been supplied with a bread knife, it is not to be used to cut the bread, except at breakfast or teatime. Bread or rolls are broken, not cut. Break a little off at a time, apply butter if necessary, the butter having been deposited first on your side plate, and pop in the mouth. Splitting a roll with a knife and layering it with butter smacks rather of a sandwich-maker at a deli counter.

♦ Pips, stones and bones have to be dealt with and one cannot be expected to swallow them. There is a school of etiquette which suggests a subtle transfer from mouth to fork, to plate. A really deft touch is needed for this tricky operation. Fish bones are easy but pips and stones impossible. The way to transfer them from mouth to plate is via a semi-closed fist. Expel them into fist, thumb uppermost, and place them on the plate.

- Smoking is dealt with separately under 'Smoking', however suffice it to say smokers should not light up until all food has been cleared away. At formal banquets they are given the go-ahead when the Master of Ceremonies announces after the toasts, 'Ladies and gentlemen, you may now smoke'. Cigarettes, cigars and matches are then passed around, and ash trays laid. At private parties, discretion and sensitivity are called for.

- Special dietary requirements. At the risk of being called a crank it is important to indicate to one's host if there are foods that one cannot eat. It is unfair to the hosts to stay mum and then return each dish untouched. That thought must have been what prompted an American banker, who was joining an Irish house party, to send a long list of his forbidden foods. They included beef, ham and all pig produce, meat cooked with dairy products and shell fish. The hosts anticipated a Muslim and welcomed a Jew. Religious restrictions spring from common sense and hygiene practices used in hot countries in pre-refrigeration days.

- Eating fruit can pose a problem at formal meals. On very grand occasions it can be touched only with a knife and fork. Bananas are the best fruit for beginners. All one has to do is top and tail the banana on the plate, then run a knife along the skin lengthways, follow this with another confident cut about an inch away. The peel can then easily come away and the fruit can be cut as required. In the interests of hygiene, apples and pears should be peeled. It is best to halve, quarter and core the fruit first, but remember it should not leave the plate for the hand during the operation. Grape and cherry stones are removed as previously indicated.

- Melons are served in wedges and eaten with a spoon, or more commonly with a knife and fork. Pomegranates, passion fruit, kiwi and other similar fruits are halved and the flesh scooped out with a small spoon.

- When eating game, take care not to get a mouthful of shot. Biting the bullet can cause shooting pains in tooth fillings.
- Kebabs are not eaten directly from the skewer. Run a fork down the skewer first to remove pieces.
- Caviar and pâté are eaten on toast. Hot toast for pâté, cold (or blinis) for caviar. Sometimes chopped onion and hardboiled egg are offered with caviar.
- Toothpicks are often placed on restaurant tables, but all picking or prodding of orifices is best done in private.

Eating Out

E ating out does not mean eating in the street, an unacceptable habit for which there is no etiquette, but unfortunately a custom on the increase in New York and probably in other U.S. cities also. Munching a hot dog or pretzel has become acceptable practice (not to me), but the line has to be drawn at eating a two- or three-course meal while walking as many blocks.

It is not an unusual sight in lunchtime Manhattan to see a young executive walking along with his deli tray in one hand, his fork in the other and a mobile phone balanced between ear and shoulder This writer may have given the impression of being averse to mobile telephones in public places — she is! She is also against chewing on the sidewalk. The fact that all these mobile lunchers are young suggests that either chronic indigestion knocks them out at an early age or that they eventually graduate to expense account tables.

Picnics

Picnics fall into two categories, the traditional family picnic which is of the moist tomato-sandwiches-and-warm-lemonade school, or the more formal cold pheasant-and-chilled-wine variety. All picnic food tastes heavenly to this picnic lover provided it does not come in plastic. Nature is too magnificent to insult with plastic knives and forks. Furthermore, to insult a bottle of wine with plastic, or worse, paper cups is unforgivable.

Setting the scene for a picnic is as important as the food itself. Obviously the chosen spot has everything that the picnickers desire, be it a place of spectacular beauty, or within proximity of public lavatories, or the grassy splendour of an outdoor opera festival. The writer's finest picnic was enjoyed at a gala musical event; the food has slipped my mind, all I can remember is that we drank from crystal glasses and the dusk was candlelit by a spectacular candelabra. This may appear a bit over the top for the average Sunday afternoon jaunt, however the memory of dining off china and drinking from crystal remains. I grant that children's picnics call for simpler measures, although little people also appreciate the finer things in life — but only if introduced to them.

The one essential for all picnic food is that it should be easy to eat. Health-conscious muesli eaters travel with great bowls of green and red leaves coated *in situ* with an amusing little French dressing. Now large-leaved salads are not easy to tackle when seated at a table, but in the open they really do resemble rabbit food. Salads should come in manageable, bite-sized pieces, likewise slices of rare roast beef. Quiches have the advantage of being easy to eat but the disadvantage of becoming as soggy as the aforementioned tomato sandwiches. Cold pheasant is eaten with the fingers, but as it is relatively dry this shouldn't pose too great a problem. Spanish potato omelettes, which are the sophisticated equivalent of the traditional hard-boiled egg, travel extremely well and are easy to eat. For 'afters' chocolate is a bad bet as it melts in the hamper (only a hamper please!), in the hand and on the face. A perennial favourite is rich fruit cake. Some delicate palates like to finish off with strawberries in champagne: fine, but the only way to eat them is to have them dropped into one's mouth while supine.

For children anything goes, and it usually does, as more food is dropped than eaten, making a large damp towel the most important accessory at many picnics. The only etiquette essential on picnics is to enter into them in a spirit of enjoyment. Rain, insects, and soggy food are all part of life's rich tapestry.

Restaurant Eating

'Restaurants have this in common with ladies: the best are often not the most enjoyable, nor the grandest the most friendly, and the pleasures of the evening are frequently spoiled by the final writing of an exorbitant cheque.' (John Mortimer)

Good manners in a restaurant is a two-sided affair — a social contract entered into by waiter and diner. The first essential to remember when dining in a restaurant is never let the place, or more importantly, the waiter intimidate. Always bear in mind who is paying for food and service. A waiter is there to take the orders, serve, and receive complaints, compliments and tips; he is also a fellow human being doing a job. There is a rather obnoxious type of diner that faded empires throw up, who regard waiters, even ex-waiters, with complete disdain.

A story told of Nicholas Soames in the House of Commons illustrates this point. John Prescott, a fellow M.P., had once served as a steward in the Merchant Navy, a fact Soames and his cohorts would not let him forget. Every time Prescott stood up, he was greeted with a chorus of drink orders, and a loud 'Same again Giovanni' from Soames.

Eating out can be traumatic if the waiter is rude, the food abominable and the bill astronomical: then again it can be a few hours of bliss, cheap at the price. Life is a gamble.

Restaurant Hosts

Booking in advance is essential in most good restaurants, and even in lesser places it is to be recommended as a means of introducing oneself to the staff. Booking is even more necessary if a woman is the host, particularly for business entertaining. Not only should she book in advance but also take the trouble to specify the table required. In an unknown restaurant this may not be possible so the keen executive will check out the place first to make sure that her party will not be seated either half-way into the kitchen or the gentlemen's lavatory. This booking visit also ensures that the head waiter and wine waiter know who is host and to whom the bill goes. Of course there should not be different rules for men and women, but life is not all it should be, certainly not in restaurants or on aircraft.

When taking out a friend, or group of friends to a restaurant they are unfamiliar with, it is advisable to give them an idea of the dress code. If the restaurant insists on jacket and tie, it's best to let them know in advance rather than have them turned away in designer jeans and leather. Business entertaining makes slightly more demands on the inviting host (see Business Entertaining, page 115).

Drinks Beforehand

'After four martinis, my husband turns into a disgusting beast. After the fifth, I pass out altogether.' (Anon.)

A host always arrives before the guests. They are greeted on arrival, coats taken, and drinks ordered if they choose to remain at the bar. Going to the bar should always be the diner's decision. Sometimes, at night, a long wait is foisted on diners due to over-booking. Whereas this is unacceptable there is little one can do other than drink one's dinner (as the above quote from Anon. suggests), or leave there and then. There should be no reason to wait at lunchtime and many hosts prefer to go straight to the table and greet the guests from there.

Waiting to be Seated

The American custom of a barrier, behind which diners must wait until seated by a hostess or head waiter can provoke feelings of mutiny. On this side of the Atlantic we are not quite as docile. The custom is to stand like an obedient hound who has been told 'wait', despite the fact that most of the tables are unoccupied. The hostess disappears, writes her autobiography, composes a full-length opera or paints the Sistine Chapel before returning to her lengthening line of obedient labradors. Perhaps this is known as restaurant training. When you are eventually guided to a table, gratitude, even a tip, is expected. This guide on etiquette would be in favour of well-mannered revolt against this custom. Who is paying the bill? Are we mice (or dogs) or men?

Unlike the rest of us impatient people, Celia puts her queueing time to good use. Her house is awash with petit point cushion covers representing many hours spent in line. Not only does she produce an end product but she also eliminates tension.

Seating

If you have not pre-booked a specific table and you are shown to one that you dislike, and there are other tables available, do make your preference known. Unfortunately in restaurants the meek neither inherit the earth nor get the best tables. It is the custom for the host to give himself the least attractive seat, either facing away from the action or in the passage-way. Women are traditionally given the better seats on the banquettes (a type of inequality of which I am all in favour). The rigid division of sexes is not as strictly adhered to in restaurants as it is at formal dinner parties. If the party is small and the women prefer to sit facing the men, that is not a break with etiquette, provided they have the better seats!

Menus and Ordering

Some smart restaurants have separate menus for hosts and guests, with no prices on the guests' menus. It has been said that this can be a cause of embarrassment to a guest who is nervous of ordering items of unknown cost. Nonsense! There are few people in this day and age who do not realise that there is a price differential between caviar and black pudding, or foie gras and chef's salad. The Very Charming Guest will ask the host to suggest something, thus deftly getting out of the situation while acknowledging the delighted host's superior knowledge. How can they lose?

The next hurdle is which menu to choose from as most restaurants present table d'hôte and à la carte. The first is the shorter daily fixed menu, the second offers a much larger selection at an appreciably higher price. In steps the good host murmuring 'do have whatever you like' but he may not intend unlimited munificence. A discerning guest will wait for the hint, which is either 'I am going to go with the table d'hôte, they do a really interesting menu here', or 'Let's try the à la carte, the lobsters are flown in daily and are quite superb'. Lucky guest, price is clearly of no consequence.

Rosemary was a perfect guest and always chose the least expensive item on the menu — an omelette. As she was dating an impecunious barrister at the time everyone assumed it was because of cost. 'Not at all,' Rosemary explained, 'it is in case he asks me a question when my mouth is full, an omelette is easiest to swallow.' They got married, he is now one of the high earners at the bar and she still eats omelettes!

If the meal is Dutch and separate bills are required it is best to request them before the waiter has filled out his order pad. If the restaurant is not too happy about this — tough! If they refuse because of staff inconvenience, find somewhere that will offer service which is convenient to the customer. In fairness to the restaurant that objects, separate bills within a large group who are drinking quantities of alcohol, or eating a complicated, multi-order Chinese meal, can prove very difficult to execute. Large parties who intend to eat and drink with abandon would be well advised to bring along their own accountant.

Ordering should be done through the host in deference to his position. Not so long ago female guests never addressed the waiter, every request being made through the man. In those far off days of discreet service, neither the host nor the waiter referred to the woman guest as anything other than 'Madam'. The man relayed the order as 'Madam will have the oysters and then the lamb cutlets', and likewise the man was never addressed as anything but 'Sir'. Nowadays familiarity with address has gone far enough, if not too far. Consider this example: 'Well, if it isn't Mr Brown, we haven't seen you for an age.' If Mr Brown is with his wife whom he has told that the reason he has been missing from the table at home all week is because he had to entertain in this restaurant, that man is in trouble. Or, how about the waiter who greeted a regular customer, lunching with a lady who was not his wife, with, 'Good afternoon Mr O'C. and how is Mrs O'C.?' Quick as a flash our cute customer replied, 'My mother is well thank you'.

When the waiter arrives, pad in hand, the host rallies his guests for their orders. As with a sinking ship, the custom was for the women to go first. However, with a large party it may be more convenient for the waiter to ignore this custom and take each order in turn around the table. Such a practice, although not strictly adhering to past etiquette, is really quite acceptable.

The host is still on duty after the food arrives at table and should check that each guest has received what they wanted, and that it is to their satisfaction. If a guest has to call a waiter directly, it indicates that the host is not paying enough attention. No matter what a guest needs they should never make a direct request in the dining-room or bar of a private club.

The Menu

If in doubt regarding a dish, do consult the waiter, via the host of course. Although the international language of food is French, menus in ethnically-varied restaurants come in a variety of languages. There is no problem if the waiter speaks your language — if not, rely on a dictionary. Do not emulate poor David who spent two weeks travelling throughout the Czech Republic and to this day has no idea what he ate. Consulting the waiter for an explanation is perfectly understandable but asking a waiter's advice as to what one should eat is ludicrous. In fact, requesting a recommendation often means that you are given whatever dish the kitchen is trying to 'push' that day. Stating however that you would like to eat fish and will choose from the selection whatever is fresh and wild, is a sensible request. If, after the customer has taken the waiter's advice, what arrives is both frozen and farmed, he has every justification in sending the dish back.

Waiters in General, Head Waiters in Particular

'By and by,

God caught his eye.' (David McCord)

Certainly only God could catch the eye of some waiters. Other methods employed to catch an elusive waiter's attention are a raised hand or a raised voice, but the voice must only be slightly raised as waiters can be very touchy creatures. Whistling, clicking the fingers or clapping hands are all frowned on today. In the Fifties in Spain the hand-clapping method was universally employed, and with remarkable success I may add. A snap of the fingers might appear derogatory, but who could object to applause? In the face of attempting to get attention today via facial contortions, stiff right arms and plaintive cries for help — re-introduce the clap I say!

Managing to get table water in restaurants rates up there beside an expectation that the Revenue Commissioners will return excess monies paid. Bills are the next most difficult item to obtain, but here the solution is simple: just stand up and head for the door and you will hold the attention of the entire staff.

The only thing worse than no attention is too much attention. So Kevin found during a business dinner in one of London's finer hotels. The waiters returned to the table so frequently with unwanted offerings, or that put-your-teeth-on-edge request 'Is everything alright?', that eventually Kevin had to call the head waiter and request to be left alone.

The less expensive the restaurant the more effusive the waiter. Trendy establishments favour the 'Hi, my name is John, I'm looking after you today' approach. This approach is liked by some and loathed by others: the dividing line may well be the generation gap. These same restaurants also offer a long recitation of the menu. Demanding such concentration of paying customers is a bit much — best to confess amnesia and have it all written down, with the prices. Over-friendly waiters are really a hazard of the New World. French waiters exhibit all the natural reticence of their race when dealing with foreigners.

The better the restaurant the less obvious the service. Waiters appear is if by magic when there is a lull in the conversation, or to replace a dropped implement. They remember who has ordered which dish. There is none of that standing plate in hand, saying, 'Who's the salmon?' Neither will a first-class restaurant place a full plate in front of a customer; except for soup, food should be proffered on a salver and then served.

Attention to detail is illustrated by the probably apocryphal story of the commis waiter who was castigated severely by his head waiter for wielding a silver serving spoon with great dexterity to pop the slippage in a lady's cleavage back in place. 'But Sir,' said the waiter 'you wouldn't have expected me to use my hands.' 'Not at all,' was the reply 'but, young man, in this establishment we always heat the spoon first.'

This side of the Atlantic head waiters are a relatively unflamboyant lot. How very different it is in the United States, where known as maître d', an abbreviation of maître d'hôtel, they are for many the ultimate social arbiters. Being recognised by them is the lifelong ambition of many a New York socialite. The writer Erica Jong describes her idea of a Jewish heaven as having a name 'that cows maître d's'. In a city where having the right table tells the whole story, control of these tables means power. It is up to the maître d' to decide when a client has graduated to a power table, and worse, to dictate the searing moment of the down-grading. Folding money, discreetly passed, can help: tipping is one of the things that keeps the Big Apple turning.

Complaining

The world is unevenly divided between the docile and the complainers. Complainers may not be popular, but they get what they want.

Some complaints to waiters are more than justified, others are intended to be passed on to the kitchen. Direct complaints to waiters concern service; if the service is too slow a request for speedier attention should bring results. If not, one can always try U.S. etiquette guru Miss Manners' method, which involves a judicious request for a telephone to be brought to the table. She then asks for the number of the kitchen, explaining politely that she is just enquiring what is the matter. Failing that, she will request the number of a good take-away in the area.

Another clear area for complaint is the nasty habit employed by too many waiters today of clearing the table before the entire party has finished eating. Good manners decree that no plates be removed until the last straggler lays down their knife and fork.

Complaints about the quality of the food are less clear cut. If the food is not what was ordered, or not at the correct temperature, or indeed if not of a suitable standard, the waiter should be notified. A top-class waiter will sweep the plate away without argument and offer to correct or replace the dish. Arguing with a customer is not acceptable. If the dish is not satisfactory there should be no discussion about it. A debating society and not a restaurant is the place for discussion. If the waiter shows an inclination to either, call the manager, or leave.

A word of warning from the other side of the table: unreasonable and loudly-voiced complaints can put the kitchen staff's hackles up. So if sending back a dish, do so at your peril. Heaven knows what subtle and illicit flavours may be added to the dish in transit.

Paying the Bill

Restaurants which offer a second sitting are irritatingly punctual with their bills; otherwise, as already mentioned, bills can be more difficult to extract than wisdom teeth. The universal sign for 'bill please' is a handwriting-in-the-air gesture, when you have caught the waiter's eye. There are few restaurants who disguise their bills under a silver cover, in an antique box or between the petals of a flower. A reliable rule of thumb is — the more elaborate the disguise, the more outrageous the ransom demanded. The original hide-the-bill performance was to prevent sensitive guests from seeing the total; doubling the bill over is quite satisfactory.

Credit cards come into their own in restaurants, being even more discreet than cheques. A wise precaution when paying by credit card is to ascertain that the final total has been filled in. It is frequently left open to facilitate the adding of a tip. When paying by cash it is unseemly to count it out at table.

Tipping varies greatly and it is therefore difficult to offer a general guideline. Sometimes it is included in the bill, sometimes not. If the service has been exceptional, a tip may well be left on top of the service charge. Some big tippers buy their restaurant popularity; others over tip out of embarrassment, and then there are the misers. The acceptable norm is between 10% and 15% although in the U.S. it can go up to 20%. Tipping is apportioned between all waiting staff which means the sommelier (wine waiter) will receive a percentage of the wine bill.

Wine Waiter or Sommelier

'When it came to writing about wine, I did what almost everyone does — I faked it.' (Art Buchwald)

The wine waiter or *sommelier* is the one with the chain around his neck. Sometimes the chain may have a key on it to indicate the key of the cellar, but more commonly it carries a flattish silver cup known as *tasse de vin* (tasting cup) which is the tool of his trade. He or she is the person who proffers the wine list and is there to advise or suggest. Once the choice is made, he fetches the bottle, shows it to the host and opens it at the table, leaving the cork with the host. The next step is to pour a little into the host's glass for tasting. Experienced wine buffs or 'grapies' use their nose for this part of the ceremony.

Corked wine smells foul and tastes worse. Wine is tasted not to sample the flavour or confirm the choice but to ensure that it is drinkable and at the correct temperature. Corked wine does not mean little pieces of cork floating around the glass but a rotten cork which has let the air in and turned the wine. It is a rare occurrence and impossible to overlook — unless one is a regular meths drinker. The taste of the wine is a matter of choice for the diner: the condition of it is the restaurant's responsibility.

If a white wine is not chilled enough, it is best to advise the waiter to pour just a little into each glass and place the bottle in an ice bucket. It is wiser to hold on to a red wine that is too chilled as sending it back means an attempt might be made to raise the temperature at speed and this could ruin the wine. House wine should not be tasted.

Following the tasting ritual the waiter pours the wine into each guest's glass, ladies first. A host should ascertain what guests are eating before ordering wine. In general, white wine goes best with fish and red with meat. Sometimes both are ordered, white to start with followed by red. The wine waiter refills the glasses (never more than half way) as required — a host can do this also. But guests who help themselves look greedy and waiters who insist on topping up the glass after every sip look as if they are touting for business.

Champagne

It is possible to drink champagne right through the meal although some might consider it a little light and airy for meat. Carol, who was relatively new to champagne and a self-declared trend setter, declared that vintage champagne was the only drink to accompany her late-night plate of chips — all too soon she became an overweight bankrupt.

> Here's to champagne, the drink divine
> That makes us forget our troubles
> It is made of a dollar's worth of wine
> And three dollars' worth of bubbles. (Anon.)

Champagne comes in many sizes. As well as the one and a half glass snipe, the half bottle and the bottle, there are:

The magnum	=	2 bottles
The jeroboam	=	4 bottles
The rehoboam	=	6 bottles
The Methuselah	=	8 bottles
The Nebuchadnezzar	=	20 bottles

Business Entertaining

Business entertaining comes under myriad headings: access to new clients, massaging old ones, interviewing or rewarding staff, or the blending of two sympathetic expense accounts. Setting the scene by booking a specific table and how to pay tactfully have already been dealt with. Clever executives will have established themselves at a selection of restaurants in different price categories. The host can then match the restaurant to the guest. The perfect host always leads the way in letting the guest know what price range to choose from and never forces alcohol when it is refused by someone returning to an office to work — unless, of course, the guest is a serious rival.

If the necessity arises to cancel a business meal, it is done directly on a person-to-person level; apologising through secretaries is not the act of the well-mannered business person. A wise precaution is to confirm on the day with both restaurant and guest. Likewise a guest who does not receive a confirmation should check it out also.

Punctuality is to be hoped for on every occasion: at a business meal it is essential. To belittle a colleague through a callous disregard for their time is unforgivable. Some unpunctual souls feel that leaving a message of late arrival at the restaurant absolves them — it doesn't. It does however alleviate their companion's fear of having arrived at the wrong place on the wrong day.

Some Don'ts for Restaurant-goers

- Do not take children to a restaurant unless they know how to behave. Ruining other diners' meals is unacceptable. This writer is all for taking little people out to dine in public — otherwise how will they ever learn restaurant behaviour? However, it is the behaviour of accompanying parents that is often a cause for concern. They have a responsibility to control their offspring in public places. Children find sitting still impossible and there are two methods of dealing with fidgeters — they can be distracted and entertained by the parent, or they can be bound and gagged. The first method could be considered good manners, the second, child abuse. A surprisingly large section of the community would be in favour of separate sections for children in aircraft and restaurants.

- Do not table hop, always the sign of an *arriviste*. 'Selling raffle tickets' was how a perceptive people-watcher described it. Table hoppers not only desert their own companions but manage to unsettle each table they visit. Conversation and eating are suspended and the men have to rise if it is a woman. On seeing a friend in a restaurant, a smile or a wave of the hand is sufficient. There is no need to turn a brief encounter into 'Surprise Surprise'.
- Do not help yourself to the food on your neighbour's plate; neither is it polite to feed others around the table from your own plate. Be discreet, if exchanging samples, and put the morsel on the other's plate or side dish.
- Do not speak on the telephone when at table.
- Do not light up in a non-smoking area, or when the rest of the company is still eating.
- Do not cover the table with either business papers or bulky handbags.
- Do not apply make-up at table.
- Do not use a tooth-pick at table, even if it is supplied.

PART TWO

Hatches
Matches
Despatches

Births

The Announcement

First step after a birth is to rejoice. Every new arrival should be a cause for joy, a joy that parents, and especially grandparents, want to share with the world by putting an announcement in the newspaper.

Short and simple is the favoured style for birth announcements:

Brown: on 22nd June 199- at the Rotunda Hospital, Dublin,
to John and Mary (née Bloggs)*, a son (Kevin John)*.

* This additional information is optional, but inclusion is customary.

Then there are the announcements which include grateful thanks to the doctor, delivery unit, and half the hospital, as well as including the names of previous offspring. The longer the entry, the greater the cost: it is entirely a matter of taste. The tradition for all personal newspaper announcements is to give the facts only.

In the case of a single parent, the notice would read:

Bloggs: on 22nd June 199- at the Rotunda Hospital, Dublin,
to Mary a son.

Even simpler would be:

Bloggs: on 22nd June 199- to Mary, a son.

Unmarried couples give their names and indicate what surname the child will use:

Bloggs: on 22nd June 199- at the Rotunda Hospital, Dublin,
to Mary and John Brown, a son.

119

Women who insist on using their own name on such occasions can cause confusion. Adoptive parents like to insert the words 'by adoption'.

The Christening

Before the christening comes the State registration of the newly arrived citizen with the State. Medical staff are very helpful in advising on this procedure.

Catholic christenings tend to take place earlier than Church of Ireland (or England) services. Some parents prefer to wait until their children can walk to the font, making the traditional holding of the child by the godmother a veritable weight-lifting feat.

GODPARENTS

Godparents can play an important role in a child's life. Apart from the gifts they give, they should be prepared to care for the spiritual welfare of their charge, and in some cases, on the death of a parent, assume the role of guardian. It is wise therefore to select people with an outlook on life that one would like one's child to share.

A request to act as godparent should not be taken lightly. The role can be onerous, but the request itself is a great compliment, and one not to be refused carelessly. The difficulty arises in knowing how to refuse without giving offence. A refusal on the basis of a difference of religion, or a complete lack of one, is not sufficient cause; neither is absence, as stand-ins known as proxies can be used. The only let-out is the plea of having filled one's quota of godchildren. This is an understandable excuse but may still put a severe strain on a friendship. The wise parent tests the waters to make sure of an acceptance before plunging in, and by doing so avoids embarrassment all around. Two godparents, a man and a woman, are sufficient for a Catholic christening, whereas in the Church of Ireland they require at least three. Boys have two godfathers and one godmother, girls the reverse. There is a certain enviable lavishness about a line up rather than a modest pair.

THE SERVICE

The service is short. The godparents stand around the font, mother handing the child over to the principal godmother. Even the most experienced is overcome by the 'what if' sensations at this point: 'What if I drop him/her in the water?' Relax, it has not happened yet.

During the brief service the godparents respond to the clergyman on the child's behalf and enunciate the name clearly when requested. Moyra Bremner, in *Enquire Within* recounts the incident of the child christened Spindonna. Apparently when the clergyman requested her name, the Scottish father replied, 'It's pinned on her'.

A form of service popular in the Catholic church is the communal christening. Weekend Mass in some parishes is followed, or preceded, by group christenings, a shared community experience. The author supposes that there is much to be said for multiple services, but she isn't prepared to say it. She has no more intention of sharing a church ceremony than she has of sharing a hospital bed.

THE RECEPTION

Christenings are intimate family affairs, shared with the godparents and a few close friends. The traditional form of entertainment would be a small reception with champagne, some nibbles and a christening cake, or a luncheon party. One of the most enjoyable christenings in recent years was a sit-down luncheon for forty followed by fiddlers and dancing. The highlight of the party is the cutting of the cake, and the godfather's (or godmother's) toast to the baby. The cake can be decorated with the baby's initials. Couples often retain one layer of their wedding cake for this purpose.

CHRISTENING GIFTS

Attendance at a christening does not require a present. But it is best to bring some small item rather than stand out as a skinflint if everyone else turns up bearing gifts. It is customary for the godparent's gift to be something of lasting value. Some choose to open a bank account in the baby's name and add to it at Christmas and birthdays, others might lay down some wine or port. A pipe of port was considered a suitable gift for a godson, to be broken into on the occasion of his twenty first birthday, a generous gift indeed as a pipe contains one hundred and five gallons. Silver in the form of spoons or a mug is popular, as are cuff links or a simple piece of jewellery for a girl.

WHAT TO WEAR

The baby, the star of the show, wears a long white dress, irrespective of sex. Traditionally this fine lawn and lace christening robe is handed down from one generation to the next and as it is worn for only a few hours by a tiny, immobile creature it can remain in perfect condition for decades. If there is not a christening robe already in the family, the heirloom can begin with this generation. Over the dress goes a warm shawl.

Older children being christened tend to wear white also, or something more practical but still in a light colour. The rest of the party wear Sunday best, with hats for the ladies.

The Engagement
and the Wedding

‘If it were not for the presents an elopement would be preferable.’ (George Ade)

These are hardly the correct sentiments in which to enter the state of matrimony. But let's face it, a wedding has very little to do with marriage. It is a family occasion, a celebration, an opportunity to return hospitality to friends and relatives. It is also a highly expensive form of entertainment and all those wedding presents help put some of the gilt back on the gingerbread.

When is the best time to get married? Whenever it suits you. June and Christmas are reckoned to be the most popular times. One cynic, when asked, replied 'After the divorce and before the birth'.

The Engagement

First comes the engagement. Etiquette here suggests that the groom-to-be asks, consults, or at least informs the father of the bride-to-be of his intentions. The man presents the woman with a ring, although customs differ from country to country — in Spain it is a bracelet. Families and friends are given the glad tidings. Good manners and a sense of self-preservation indicate that former lovers should also be notified. In the case of Lothario-about-town Nicholas this essential was overlooked. The ex-lovers (there were quite a few) only learned about their newly-acquired 'ex' status upon reading the engagement announcement. They were not pleased. Two of the discarded ladies conveyed their displeasure to the bride-to-be, with some unkind personal remarks about

Nicholas. A less verbal ex-lover dumped his clothing and C.D.s at
the bride's home. The moral of this tale is — before announcing an
engagement, tie up all loose ends.

Some couples feel that a personal notification of their
engagement to family and friends is sufficient: a large number prefer
to make a public announcement in the newspaper. There is a
traditional form of announcement, which runs as follows:

> MR I.B. JONES
> MISS M.A. BLOGGS
> The engagement is announced between
> Ian Brian, eldest son of Mr and Mrs
> B.C. Jones of Gorey, Co. Wexford,
> and Mary Ann, only daughter of
> Mr and Mrs T.P. Bloggs, of Ranelagh,
> Dublin 6.

In the case of deceased or divorced parents, it could read.

> MR I.B. JONES
> MISS M.A. BLOGGS.
> The engagement is announced between
> Ian Brian, eldest son of Mr B.C. Jones
> and the late Mrs Jones (or Mary Jones),
> of Gorey, Co. Wexford, and Mary
> Ann, only daughter of Mr T.P. Bloggs,
> of Ranelagh, Dublin 6 and Mrs M.D.
> Second-Time, of The Harem,
> Enniskerry, Co. Wicklow.

There are some amazing examples of originality in forthcoming
marriage announcements in Irish newspapers. The more formal
merely change around the wording of preceding examples. The
insertions by the couples themselves tend to be brief and enigmatic,
and appear to be aimed only at their own families and inner circle.
They read:

> DR MARY BLOGGS
> JOHN JONES B.A.
> John and Mary, together with
> their families, are happy to
> announce their engagement.

There is nothing incorrect here; etiquette is only a guideline in these matters. The only problem is that both Jones and Bloggs, as well as John and Mary, are quite common names. Only the inner circle can be sure that it is an offspring of their Bloggs or Jones who is about to get hitched. It may be that John and Mary wish to remain relatively anonymous and not have to deal with letters, tokens or congratulations.

Another, less used style of announcement might suit the same John and Mary better. It reads:

MISS MARY BLOGGS
MR JOHN JONES
The engagement is announced
and the marriage will shortly
take place between Mr John
Jones, Gorey, Co. Wexford and
Miss Mary Bloggs, Ranelagh,
Dublin 6.

Then there are couples who prefer to announce only the wedding. Into this category fall the more mature lovers, ones with multiple spouses already, elopements, shotgun weddings, marriages taking place abroad, or the anti-social. (See examples of these wedding announcements on page 129.) The major handicap to a trouble-free trot up the aisle is a former marriage. A tricky one this, particularly in Ireland. Regardless of how well-behaved the participants, good manners are over-ruled by State laws on this one. Divorce is not the only impediment to union, and there are other laws which may not be quite so familiar to those bent on matrimony. These are known as the Table of Prohibited Degrees of Kindred and Affinity.

Almost every male toddler promises to marry his mother when he grows up. On the off-chance that as an adult he still has the same sense of commitment he would do well to study the following list. Whereas it would be a rare odd-ball that would contemplate marriage with a grandparent, some of the other prohibited unions seem all too easy to imagine, such as those between step relatives and in-laws. Best to read through it before putting in the announcement.

'Table of Prohibited Degrees of Kindred and Affinity' (*Digest of Irish Family Law*)

Note: The relationship of the half-blood is of the same effect as relationship of the whole blood, and the Table applies to illegitimate as well as to legitimate relations.

(A Man may not marry his)

1. Grandmother	16. Sister
2. Grandfather's wife	17. Wife's Sister★
3. Wife's Grandmother	18. Brother's Wife
4. Father's Sister	19. Son's Daughter
5. Mother's Sister	20. Daughter's Daughter
6. Father's Brother's Wife	21. Son's Son's Wife
7. Mother's Brother's Wife	22. Daughter's Son's Wife
8. Wife's Father's Sister	23. Wife's Son's Daughter
9. Wife's Mother's Sister	24. Wife's Daughter's Daughter
10. Mother	25. Brother's Daughter
11. Stepmother	26. Sister's Daughter
12. Wife's Mother	27. Brother's Son's Wife
13. Daughter	28. Sister's Son's Wife
14. Wife's Daughter	29. Wife's Brother's Daughter
15. Son's Wife	30. Wife's Sister's Daughter

(A Woman may not marry her)

1. Grandfather	6. Father's Sister's Husband
2. Grandmother's Husband	7. Mother's Sister's Husband
3. Husband's Grandfather	8. Husband's Father's Brother
4. Father's Brother	9. Husband's Mother's Brother
5. Mother's Brother	10. Father

11. Stepfather	21. Son's Daughter's Husband
12. Husband's Father	22. Daughter's Daughter's Husband
13. Son	23. Husband's Son's Son
14. Husband's Son	24. Husband's Daughter's Son
15. Daughter's Husband	25. Brother's Son
16. Brother	26. Sister's Son
17. Husband's Brother	27. Brother's Daughter's Husband
18. Sister's Husband*	28. Sister's Daughter's Husband
19. Son's Son	29. Husband's Brother's Son
20. Daughter's Son	30. Husband's Sister's Son

* 'The Table of Prohibited Degrees' has been modified by the Deceased Wife's Sister's Marriage Act, 1907, which allows the marriage of a man with the sister or half sister of his deceased wife, but the Act does not extend to any other relationship.

Congratulations

If none of the above prohibitions apply congratulations are in order but be careful, it is a word to be used with caution. Good manners require that only the man be congratulated — presumably on achieving such a prize after a long and difficult chase — whereas his demure, wouldn't-know-how-to-set-a-trap partner is wished 'every happiness'.

Further formalities such as engagement parties are at the discretion of the couple and their families. It was the custom for family friends, godparents or relatives to invite them to dinner. This probably still holds good in circles with servants. It is, however, customary for the two families to have a get together — 'sizing up the opposition' is how one harrassed bride described it. There is a simple solution to the two camp syndrome and that is to marry a distant cousin. The most relaxed and enjoyable wedding I ever attended was between two third cousins. Any eccentric or difficult relatives (and don't we all have them) were a joint responsibility shared equally by the bride, the groom, and the majority of the guests.

The Wedding

The bible admonishes, 'It is better to marry than to burn': a suggestion on a par with 'Old age is preferable to the alternative'. Despite the ridicule heaped on the institution — it is the second most popular butt of jokes after mothers-in-law — marriage is here to stay. It is only the opening chapter we deal with here. Wedding etiquette remains the same, be the wedding big or small; errors, however, are magnified by numbers. The first step is to arrange for church, reception and guest list.

GUEST LIST

In making out the guest list a rough estimate is normally agreed upon by the very reasonable sets of parents and the two main participants. The wise will tell you that the estimate and the reality have little in common. Families have more complicated branches than a monkey puzzle tree, and even the most anti-social appear to have a limitless number of close friends. How not to invite without giving offence is a question to which nobody has found an answer. There are various underhand methods, such as franking all the invitations together and 'forgetting' to mail some. Good manners prevent any comments on these matters. However experience has shown that the best method to employ is the 'grin and bear it' one. Quite apart from the fact that some of the dreaded guests may prove themselves valued friends in years to come, in this life our principal regrets are for what we did not do rather than what we did.

INVITATIONS AND ANNOUNCEMENTS

For a standard wedding invitation, see page 13.

WEDDING ANNOUNCEMENTS

A custom prevalent in the United States and continental Europe is the sending out of announcement cards after the wedding. The warm glow which a wedding invitation engenders is somewhat dimmed when one realises that the event has already taken place.

The reason for these announcements would appear to be to let far-flung relatives and friends, those unlikely or unable to attend the celebrations, know of the event. One is tempted to suggest that if the far-flung folk are unlikely to come, why not send them an invitation in the first place?

Couples who favour a simple intimate reception also send these little flagships out to the hundreds they would have invited had they been generous enough with their time and money to host a large reception. Whereas the thought may be pure, these cards have a faint whiff of present soliciting. Sample announcements:

> *Mr and Mrs Joseph Bloggs*
> *have pleasure in announcing*
> *the marriage of their daughter*
> *Mary to Mr Jonathan Brown*
> *which took place on Wednesday 4th June*
> *at the Pro-Cathedral, Dublin.*

If the newly-married couple wish to announce their own wedding, it would read:

> *Mary Bloggs*
> *and*
> *Jonathan Brown*
> *have pleasure in*
> *announcing their marriage*
> *which took place*
> *on Wednesday 4th June*
> *at the Pro-Cathedral, Dublin 2.*

These announcements are posted after the wedding.

POSTPONEMENTS AND CANCELLATIONS

Postponed weddings example:

> *It is much regretted*
> *that because of the*
> *death of Mrs Joseph Bloggs,*
> *the marriage between*
> *her daughter Mary*
> *and Mr Jonathan Brown*
> *on 16th April will*
> *be postponed.*
>
> 15, Thornhill Road,
> Dublin 2

Cancellation example:

> *Mr and Mrs Mrs Joseph Bloggs*
> *regret to announce that*
> *the marriage of their*
> *daughter Mary to*
> *Mr Jonathan Brown on*
> *16th April will not take place.*
>
> 15, Thornhill Road,
> Dublin 2

STAG PARTY

Once known as the bachelor dinner, stag nights are now looked upon as the last hurrah of the condemned man. Kiss-o-grams, strippers and horrendous amounts of drink put stag parties outside the remit of a book on good manners. Here it really is a case of 'every man for himself'.

Wedding Presents

Once the guest list has been agreed upon and sent out, a wedding present list (known as a Bridal Register in the United States) is usually left into selected shops. This is a practical solution to the twenty toast racks syndrome. Such a list should include a selection of gifts in all price brackets. Some expensive items can be broken up, so to speak. For example a highly-priced dinner service can be requested by place setting or even by plate. Most guests will enquire if such a list exists, or ask in the major shops. Discretion was the rule here but in the United States, where they are much more open about the whole 'wedding business' (as it is frequently described), a shop list, indeed an itemised wedding list is sometimes enclosed with the invitation. Because it is considered practical it may well become an established practice in Ireland also. However, to enclose a list of requests with an invitation is an unattractive practice and not one to be encouraged and is contrary to all tenets of Irish hospitality.

Lists left in shops should be checked on a regular basis to avoid duplication of gifts. Despite the best intentions of the couple to impress their taste and wishes on their guests, there will always be some mavericks who prefer to offer their own choice. Life would be dull without non-conformists. Some of them like to pass on family heirlooms, others their own handiwork.

It is customary that all who accept the invitation will send a gift. It is further expected that all who are invited — whether they accept or not, should do so, but this may depend on the degree of intimacy between the family and those unable to attend. Gifts are sent to the bride's home. In home receptions the gifts are displayed with the appropriate cards; in the case of cheques, they are listed, without the amount shown.

It is important to keep all cards with a note of the gift. This saves confusion when writing the thank you letters and helps flush out the cheapskates who 'forgot' to send a present. The strange law of averages decrees that the more lavish the reception the more of these turn up. The polite way to deal with such miserly amnesia is to ignore it. The other method is to telephone, and with feigned confusion confess to having mislaid some of the cards and wonder what they had given so that you can thank them properly. Underhand, yes; successful, yes.

There are couples who ask for cheques only, no gifts. This demands a very tough neck.

The Cast

For a registry office wedding the only other participants needed besides the bride and groom are the State official and two witnesses over twenty-one. For the church and more formal wedding, the bridal pair are attended by bridesmaid(s), bestman, groomsman (men) someone to give the bride away (usually a father or male relative), ushers, perhaps child attendants, officiating clergy, family and friends.

As the duties of the bestman and bridesmaid could be considered onerous, it is wise to be sure of a positive response before putting oneself, and one's friends in the embarrassing position of a refusal. If one is approached to take on such an honoured and important role it really is almost impossible to refuse without giving life-long offence. A few hours of inconvenience should be carefully weighed against the loss of a friendship. A spell in hospital or a trip to the other side of the world might be acceptable excuses.

Their duties are:

The Groom: although one of the principal participants, his role is more of a supporting one for the main performer, the bride. His duties regarding expenses and speeches are dealt with further on.

Bestman: It is his role to assist the groom, escort him to the church and hand over the wedding ring at the appropriate moment. He carries the money to take care of church donations. He is also entrusted with the groom's car and travel tickets. In the days of telegrams his was the voice that read them out, he still makes a speech at the reception and offers a toast to the bridesmaids.

Chief Bridesmaid: Matron of Honour if married. She looks after the bride, helping her prepare for the ceremony and later to change for going away. She also supervises the other bridesmaids and the child attendants, if any. During the ceremony she holds the bride's bouquet.

Father of the Bride: It is he, or a family friend or relative, who accompanies the bride to the church, walks up the aisle with her and at the altar hands her over to the groom. If he is the father of the bride he is probably parting with a great deal more than his daughter, as traditionally he pays for the reception. He also toasts the couple at the reception. (See Speeches, page 138.)

Ushers: These young men — they usually are young — help to seat people at the church. It is their duty to divide the bride and groom's party in the church. Left (facing the altar) for the bride, right for the groom. It is wise to choose friends and relatives from both sides as ushers so as to avoid the embarrassing incident witnessed when the already overwrought mother of the bride was asked — 'Bride or groom?' as she entered the church.

The old theatrical adage 'it will be alright on the night' could have been coined for wedding celebrations. Preparations for the big day can be fraught, leading to family feuds, threats of divorce (from both sets of parents), broken engagements, bankruptcy, sibling murder and nervous breakdowns.

Miraculously all disagreements are dissolved by the radiance of the bride on the big day. She is the star. All others, groom included, are merely bit players. Her father is the backer of this lavish multicast show, her mother the director. That is within the traditional mould. Nowadays working couples often bankroll their own weddings. Or, if one partner is very rich, they may insist on paying for everything, or at least sharing expenses. The inherent danger when dealing with people for whom 'money doesn't matter' is that they are notoriously forgetful about actually signing cheques. To avoid recriminations, detail the expenses beforehand.

One more point before we itemise the traditional delegation of expenses is that to remove the responsibility and expense from the bride's family may also mean removing from them dignity and enjoyment. Couples may prefer simple ceremonies with a few close friends and a minimal family representation, but think twice before causing grave and long-lasting offence.

DIVISION OF RESPONSIBILITY AND EXPENSE

Bride's family:

Wedding and engagement announcements.

Invitations.

Trousseau: Bride's and bridesmaids' dresses (if the bridesmaids have
an input into the colour and design of their dresses, they may
shoulder the expense themselves).

Floral decorations for church and reception.

Printed leaflets of order of wedding service, choir and music.

Transport for bride, bridesmaids and attendants to church
and reception.

Reception.

Wedding cake.

Photographs.

Groom:

Engagement ring.

Stag Night/Bachelor Dinner — the expenses for the evening are
usually shared among the participants.

Marriage licence.

Bouquets for bride and bridesmaids.

Buttonholes for the men in the bridal party. Plain white
carnations please.

Fees for clergy or other church expenses.

Gifts to bridesmaids.

Car for himself and bestman.

Honeymoon.

This list is rarely adhered to *in toto*. Traditions adjust, and can even
be ignored. The allocation is merely an indication of the format
employed at a time when the husband was the only, or at least, the
principal bread winner. Using this list as a yardstick may help
alleviate the tensions which inevitably arise where families and
money are involved.

What to Wear

Thankfully the Seventies and Eighties vogue for theme weddings (with everyone dolled up as cowboys and cowgirls) seems to have diminished. There is still the occasional hippy-style ceremony in flowing robes on a windswept beach. No guidelines are available for eccentricity so we shall just examine how best to turn one's self out for a traditional wedding. The custom was for the wedding to take place in the morning; the bride wore a long white dress and the men of the party wore morning clothes. The hour may be more flexible now but the dress code has remained fairly rigid. A dark lounge suit would not look amiss at any time of the day in Ireland, but would probably stand out like a soccer supporter's jersey at a formal wedding in Britain or the United States. One wonders at times if dress hire companies have discreetly taken over as social arbiters.

There are many weddings where only the bridal party, that is the groom, bestman, groomsman, ushers and parents, are expected to wear morning suit. A simple telephone call to the hosts to ascertain dress code can save embarrassment and a small fortune. Morning suits can be hired, but if you are young, marriageable and mixing with a formal wedding set, a morning suit is a sensible investment. However if morning dress is confined to the immediate wedding party, a lounge suit is quite acceptable for other male guests unless black tie is indicated (see Dress Code, page 15).

The tradition of a white dress and veil for the bride has remained fashionable for one simple reason — it is extremely flattering! The bride's dress does not have to be white, it can be cream or even a faint pink. Once upon a time white was worn to signify purity. No need to go into that now, but that was why second-time brides chose other colours, usually pastels. Red and black make quite a statement, but is it the right one?

The dress can be in any fabric, shape or design, but it is important to remember one point: the occasion lasts but a few brief hours but the photographs last for generations. A dress in the height of fashion may look ridiculous a few years hence; likewise clothes intended to amuse or shock have a brief entertainment value. Veils do wonders for women. Brides can opt for hats or flowers alone but the drift of a pale cloud up the aisle is hard to beat. The veil covers the face entering the church and frames it on leaving.

Evening weddings bring their own dress code. White tie and tails can replace morning suit for the bridal party, although black tie is more customary for guests. Female guests may dress without restraint — long dresses, jewels, tiaras if they have them. However, it is always preferable not to compete with the bride by opting for white or add too sombre a note with unrelieved black.

The same dress code can apply to a Registry Office ceremony if it is what the couple wish, but it is more customary to wear what might be termed 'Sunday Best'. This is also suitable for informal church weddings, the woman wearing a hat and the man a lounge suit (though black leather and body jewellery would not be unheard of either). In some cases where the bride and groom choose to dress up, they would prefer to spare their guests the cost of hiring.

The only clear rule that good manners insist upon in the matter of dress is to inform guests clearly what they are expected to wear; vagueness does nobody any favours. If unsure, as already stated, invitees should simply telephone and ask. No matter how unconventional the wedding, the message should be clear.

The Reception

Custom was that weddings took place in the morning followed by a wedding breakfast. The reception now takes place any time that ties in with the registry office or church ceremony. Receptions can vary from a jolly, boozy breakfast with a couple of close friends to standing for hours nibbling canapés amidst a cast of hundreds.

Luncheon is popular. However, the parsimonious favour an elaborate cocktail party in the late afternoon or 'grazing' as it is known in the United States. It is not really polite to hint that other nations might be less generous in their hospitality than the Irish, but it's true!

An increasingly popular time for the ceremony is late afternoon, followed by a dinner reception. It has much to recommend it: tardiness is less in evidence as most guests are awake by 5 p.m; the bride and her attendants have an entire day for beauty preparations; the guests avoid the post-wedding pre-party hangover, and the hosts do not have to organise extra entertainment for the evening. Separate invitations to the dinner only may be sent for this type of reception, or when the church is too small to hold the numbers invited to the reception. Whatever the time of the wedding, most couples like to make a day of it. Not Tony. Tony was one of the leading hairstylists of the Seventies. On the morning of his wedding he worked in his salon as usual. A few minutes before the ceremony he set a client in rollers, popped her under the dryer and walked around the corner to the registry office, got married, signed the relevant forms and returned in time to release the lady for a comb-out. The marriage did not last much longer than the hairstyle.

The format that the reception takes is a matter of taste and finance. The only formalities left are the speeches and cutting the cake. Whether or not to open the proceedings with a reception line is optional. If the day is wet or cold it would be more thoughtful to circulate during the reception rather than leave guests queuing outside in a hurricane.

SPEECHES

When the guests have been fed and watered, the time comes to 'say a few words'. It cannot have escaped the reader's attention that in this life those who declare themselves least adept at a task are the ones who perform it: thus it is with speeches. One only has to hear a muttered 'I'm hopeless at public speaking' to realise that a long demonstration in confirmation is about to follow. It has been remarked that like ladies' skirts, speeches should be long enough to cover the subject and short enough to be interesting.

The first speech and toast is offered by the bride's godfather, uncle or family friend. This can be undertaken by the father of the bride, but as they tend to break down under pressure it is best left to those less emotionally involved. He says a few warm words about the bride and her family, and then raises his glass to the 'Bride and Groom'.

The Groom is next in line. He responds to the toast on behalf of 'my wife and I', a remark which inevitably causes loud guffaws; he thanks the parents of his bride for entrusting her to him, thanks them also for their generous hospitality (if they are indeed the hosts); he expresses gratitude to the guests for their presence and presents, and rounds off with a toast to the bridesmaids. The more diffident and natural-sounding the groom, the more he will endear himself to his audience. This is not the moment for in-law jokes. The true professional works for weeks on an impromptu speech. Taking time to prepare can mean avoiding pitfalls. Unlike the impoverished groom who caused his guests to squirm and then titter when, in an overlong speech, he constantly referred to his heiress bride's 'sterling qualities'.

This is followed by the bestman's offering. Time was he read out the telegrams, now it is telemessages and faxes. If they are numerous a selection can be picked out — those from distant relatives and some of the more amusing ones fit for mixed company and there is no more mixed company to be found than at a wedding reception. Then he should give a short, clever and witty speech, verging on the indiscreet. Unless the bestman is a professional comedian with faultless comic timing this rarely happens. Any joke told has to avoid shocking maiden aunts and boring inebriated Rabelaisian friends. As with the groom, a well-rehearsed air of ingenuousness goes down a treat.

Here the obligatory speeches end, though most parties throw up a few spontaneous talkers. The band can be relied upon to strike up at this point.

CUTTING THE CAKE

Towards the end of the reception the wedding cake is wheeled over to the couple, or they to it. Military grooms use a sword to slice it through; this looks romantic but can be a bit messy. With a hand each on the handle of a knife the bride and groom make their incision to tremendous applause and the flash of cameras. At this stage any couple could be excused for 'believing their own publicity'.

Custom was that a layer of cake was kept and put into boxes and sent to those who could not get to the wedding; this custom appears to be dying out. Also long gone is the notion that single female guests would dream of a future husband if they placed a morsel of squashed wedding cake under their pillow — they probably believed in the tooth-fairy also. The cake is cut by the caterers and passed around with champagne. At one hotel reception where the alcohol consumption was running at over a bottle a head, and that was only the staff, two layers of the cake disappeared together with a case of champagne and four waiters. If the couple can hold on to their cake, a layer can be used at the christening.

THE END OF THE MATTER

The formalities over, the couple can depart. It has been a long, tiring and liquid day. Further over-indulgence is not to be encouraged. Take a salutary lesson from what happened to Sean. A group of vintners went to the Isle of Man on a daylong spree, known as their 'annual outing'. Come departure time strays were rounded up. One poor lad was discovered passed out in the gentlemen's lavatory and although they couldn't quite place him they guessed from his Dublin address that he was one of their own. They loaded him on to the boat bound for Dublin. On arrival the address was again sought from the still comatose body, a couple of the lads offered to drop him off. A ring on the door bell produced a middle-aged woman who agreed that Sean had indeed lived at this address but had left that morning for the Isle of Man on his honeymoon.

Wedding Anniversaries

1.	Paper	16.	Topaz
2.	Calico	17.	Amethyst
3.	Linen	18.	Garnet
4.	Silk	19.	Zircon
5.	Wood	20.	China
6.	Sugar	23.	Sapphire
7.	Floral	25.	Silver
8.	Leather	30.	Pearl
9.	Straw	35.	Coral
10.	Tin	40.	Ruby
12.	Agate	45.	Sapphire
13.	Moonstone	50.	Gold
14.	Moss Agate	55.	Emerald
15.	Rock Crystal	60.	Diamond

This list is compiled with the assistance of Weir & Sons (Dublin). There are slight variations in these lists, but the big items, such as the precious stones, gold and silver remain the same. Use your imagination to fill in the outstanding anniversaries, it is a question of desire allied to finance.

The Funeral

Ireland has a pronounced funeral culture, particularly within the Catholic Church. It is both different from, and more elaborate than that of our neighbouring island. Frequently etiquette or custom can take over when emotions become unreliable.

By the very nature of the event little time is given for advance planning. For that reason it is well to know that undertakers can take most of the strain out of making arrangements. However it might be sensible to have some ideas already in hand regarding a burial plot and religious ceremony. As people grow older they frequently want to discuss death in general with allusions to their own in particular. Cutting them off and making death a taboo subject, too depressing to be mentioned, is doing them no favours.

Some families prefer to distance themselves from all arrangements, leaving them in the hands of a solicitor or trusted family friend. Then again others want to be involved at every step of the way. This is a matter of individual taste: nothing is more personal than mourning.

If the person has died at home the doctor is the first to be notified, and a family G.P. will probably be on the alert already. The doctor's visit is essential, as without his signed death certificate no burial service can take place. The doctor can also advise on a firm of undertakers who can take over from there.

Letting People Know

A network of friends to spread the sad news and alert any who may have to make arrangements to travel, is a great help to the family. A volunteer to take over the telephone and receive messages is also a boon.

In notifying newspapers, once the wording has been agreed upon it is best to leave the insertion to the undertakers, because the newspapers will require the undertaker's verification before printing. This is to avoid bogus notices — some people's idea of a practical joke is decidedly macabre.

'Funeral private' is sometimes inserted in the notice if the bereaved prefer an intimate family gathering. In some cases a death notice is not inserted until after the interment. Other notices specify 'house private' meaning that the church is public but the house is not.

Deaths abroad are sometimes announced before the funeral arrangements are finalised, followed by a detailed announcement later.

It is difficult to give an example of an announcement, as it really is a matter of personal choice. However, the following indicates the basic format and can be added to as indicated. The address can also be included after the date:

> BLOGGS — On 4th November.
> Peacefully at home*, Michael Joseph,
> aged 84*, beloved husband of Julia
> Mary (née Brown)*, much loved father
> of John and Kevin. Removal to the
> Church of...tomorrow at 5 o'c. Funeral
> on Friday after 11 o'c Mass
> to...Cemetery.

indicates optional.

Arrangements

There are various options when arranging a burial service, particularly if it is the more elaborate Roman Catholic one. Before the service takes place however, there is the question of what to do with the body in the meantime. If a person dies in hospital their body can remain there until the coffin is taken to the church for the reception of the remains on the evening prior to the funeral, or it may be moved to a Funeral Home. The service of receiving the remains into the church is particular to the Catholic Church in Ireland. Quite apart from its religious aspect, this extra service offers mourners, who may not be able to attend a morning service, an opportunity to pay their respects.

A third choice, and one which is more frequently practised in rural areas, is to bring the body back home. In the case of a home death, the choice is to remain there or to go to a funeral parlour. It was the custom in Ireland that a dead person was waked in their own home for two days prior to funeral and interment. In this case the family and neighbours kept vigil for the forty-eight hours. Custom dictated that those who kept an all-night vigil were offered food and drink. At the end of the vigil, or the waking of the corpse, music was often played also. It should be remembered that any large gathering in rural communities has always had its social side, and as death in the Christian context is considered a departure to a better life, a celebration is not out of place. Through exaggerated practice and reports, the wake has been given a bad name, yet modern psychologists maintain that a mourning period assists the bereaved to come to terms with the trauma of death.

What to Say

It is the custom to shake hands with members of the deceased's family and murmur a few words of condolence. Silence is not acceptable no matter how tongue-tied one may feel. The usual formula or expression in this country was 'Sorry for your trouble'. It is still in use, but more often than not the shorter 'I'm sorry', or 'I'm so sorry' is used. This offering of condolence to the family used to take place outside the church following the service. Now, in urban areas at least, following the Roman Catholic ceremony on the evening prior to the funeral service, this takes place within the church. The immediate family, who sit together in the front pew of the church, remain in their seats when the service is over, and receive mourners as they file past.

As urban churches usually cater for more than one funeral in the morning, unless one is a professional mourner (or politician), it is advisable to check carefully before taking a pew. If nobody there looks familiar the chances are that it is the wrong funeral.

Male members of the family often act as pall bearers, shouldering the coffin down the aisle and later carrying it to the grave. To be asked to act as pall bearer is a singular mark of affection and respect from the family, and not one that should be lightly turned down.

Flowers and the Book of Condolence

Flowers and Mass cards are sent to the funeral home addressed to the deceased, e.g. 'The late John Brown'. They can also be brought to the church and handed to the undertakers. Names should be written clearly, preferably with surnames included, as the family will want to acknowledge the gesture. The same clarity of signature is desirable when signing the book of condolence, which the undertakers place inside the church door. In the trauma of the occasion the bereaved may forget exactly who attended but will later on wish to express their gratitude with a letter or card. Following the death of a distinguished international figure, the relevant embassy will offer a book of condolence to be signed by all who wish to express their regret and sympathy.

Regarding flowers, sheaves of cut flowers appear to be the popular choice nowadays. Wreaths tend to come from the family or from colleagues. Many a newspaper death notice states quite clearly, 'cut flowers only', or even, 'family flowers only'. A bouquet of flowers from one's own garden is often the most appreciated. Flowers are not sent in the case of Orthodox Jewish funerals.

The Burial

The majority of mourners, particularly in the city, will leave after expressing their sympathy at the church. Others will follow the funeral cortège to the cemetery by car, if the distance is long. After the hearse come the undertakers' limousines with members of the immediate family; in-laws and offspring such as grandchildren travel in the succeeding cars. There is a short service at the graveside before the body is interred. Certain areas have well-established graveyard customs, for example in south-west Ireland it would be unheard of to turn up at the cemetery without a drink for the grave diggers.

The same ritual is followed for a cremation. However sometimes, if no clear instructions have been left by the deceased, disposing of the ashes can pose a problem. Most people who request cremation leave precise instructions as to where to scatter their ashes. This happened when Desmond's wife died. Theirs was a stormy marriage, even his early widowhood being beset by storms. His wife left instructions for her ashes to be scattered over a scenic northern lough. On the appointed day a squall blew up as the boat, carrying the burial party, left land. By the time they reached the dispersal point Desmond was so nauseous that he had to lean over the edge of the boat taking in great gulps of air. It was during one of these gulps that his wife's ashes were scattered in the wind, a wind which was blowing in Desmond's direction. Even in death they were not parted.

Acknowledgment Cards and Letters

Handwritten replies to letters of condolence are the polite form. However handwriting hundreds of letters is not practical so acknowledgment cards came into being. These are printed cards which express the gratitude of the family of the deceased. They are usually distributed within the family and each member then takes care of sending them to their own friends. A polite and warm gesture is to personalise these cards with a short handwritten message. These cards can be edged in black, however black-edged and mourning stationery, so popular in Queen Victoria's day, is rarely used today.

Reception Following Funeral

It falls upon the family of the deceased to offer some hospitality to far flung friends and relatives. It is customary when receiving condolences at the church to suggest that people are welcome to call back to the house after the ceremony. One member of the family can be delegated to issue this invitation, but with clear instructions as to whether to invite only a handful or the entire congregation. A home reception is sometimes abandoned in favour of a hotel. Although not as intimate, it does relieve the family of a great deal of work. Once invited it is bad form not to make an effort to show up, if only for a short while.

Despite the sadness of the occasion, these post-funeral get-togethers can be quite enjoyable affairs. The family, united in a loss and supported by their friends, can enjoy a brief and necessary relaxation.

A reception of unbridled hilarity is not in good taste, even when it is done in the name of the deceased. 'I know John/Mary would have wanted us to have a good time.' It is improbable, or at least doubtful, that John or Mary would have been quite so altruistic regarding their farewell party. Likewise the widow who splashes around money and dances 'till dawn is not credible when she declares, 'This would have been John's wish'. It is quite probable that John would have expected at least a grieving wife, if not a nation in mourning.

Memorial Service

A memorial service is held some time after the funeral. These ceremonies are often public commemorations of a distinguished person, or they could be the home-based service for someone who was buried abroad. They differ from funerals in that they are held after the event in which case the principal character is missing. It is customary to have a friend or friends of the deceased speak during the service. Roman Catholics commemorate the deceased with a Mass one month after the funeral. This is known as the Month's Mind and is usually attended by family and close friends.

Dressing for the Occasion

During the Victorian era a period of mourning was strictly observed. The dress code was black for a number of months, then a touch of grey was introduced and later lilac. There was even mourning jewellery in the form of rings, brooches and lockets bearing a lock of the deceased's hair. In some Mediterranean countries widows remain in black for the rest of their lives, otherwise the strict protocol is only observed at court. For the rest of us the etiquette has loosened up sufficiently to permit people to make a choice.

Wearing bright clothes for the church service is still not considered good form. Inward grieving may not be apparent from the outward display, nevertheless it is regarded as a mark of respect to both the deceased and the religious ceremony to wear more sombre clothes.

Although widow's weeds with flowing veils are no longer fashionable, most widows would wear black, at least until after the interment. Men wear a plain black tie (not a dinner jacket black tie), a dark formal suit and a black armband.

PART THREE

Perfect Social Graces

Cultural Events
The Theatre

Theatre management and actors make few demands on their audience. They are as follows:

1. That the audience pay for their seats. Complimentary seats are known as 'paper seats'.
2. The grace of punctuality.
3. The stamina to remain in their seats throughout the performance. (Just imagine the dedication of the audiences of ancient Greece who sat on stone benches for hours!)
4. The ability to applaud.
5. That they are sound of wind and can sit through a performance without coughing, or 'strumming their catarrhs' as Alexander Woollcott put it.

Theatre-goers have their own requirements, which are as follows:

1. A separate section for people with long bodies: long legs are only an inconvenience to the owner but folk with long bodies sit tall.
2. Afro and all exaggerated hairstyles, as well as hats, to be forbidden.

3. Lovers should refrain from sitting 'cheek to cheek', it throws the rake behind them out of kilter. Hand-holding is permissible.
4. Kickers should have their feet tied to their seats. It is not only children who drum continuously on the back of the seat in front.
5. Any form of food or drink, with the exception of cough lozenges, should be forbidden in the auditorium. The rattle of sweetpapers can drown the actors. Drinking is now permitted in some theatres abroad, and whereas the actual drinking is not distracting, the disposal of the paper cups is.
6. The most important requirement of all is that the actors do not attempt to belittle or patronise their audience. A performance is an interplay between actor and audience. If the actors treat their audience with respect, they will receive it in return.

Regular theatre-goers are a punctual lot, experience having taught them that parking, checking in coats, buying programmes and ordering interval drinks take time. The custom of ordering the interval drinks before the performance cuts out the stampede to the bar, where one may well stand trying to catch the waiter's eye for ten of the allotted fifteen minute interval. In international theatres the average waiter to customer ratio appears to be 50/1. The ultimate in hosts will take their guest's drink order when issuing the invitation, others will order champagne or wine with the appropriate number of glasses. One regular attender brings her own in a capacious handbag.

The obvious subject for discussion at the interval is the evening's play. As a first night audience usually includes relatives of everyone connected with the performance, be wary of outspoken criticism. Careless words can hurt. The interval is also the occasion to avail of the theatre's lavatory facilities. Here the ratio of users to fixtures is even higher than that for customer/waiter — at least it is for women. The choice frequently is between the loo or a drink: to accept the second while still requiring the first can lead to bladder problems during the second act.

A bell summons the audience back to the auditorium after the interval. Once again punctuality is the virtue of princes. On one memorable occasion the bell was not sounded in one of the bars, resulting in all its occupants spilling out into the auditorium after the curtain had gone up. As chance would have it all but two were seated midway towards the back, but two unfortunates were close to the stage and directly in front of the playwright and his wife. To say he was put out would be an understatement.

The dress code for theatre has sunk to jeans and open shirts, except for opening nights when the audience makes more of an effort. Making a small effort to dress shows appreciation and respect to the performers.

BACKSTAGE ETIQUETTE

Perhaps due to the precarious nature of an actor's work the industry is riddled with superstition. Most actors laugh it off explaining that they only follow it in case they offend a fellow thespian who believes in signs and omens. Be that as it may, backstage etiquette has a rigid set of taboos. For example, whistling backstage is very bad luck. There is a reason. In bygone times the men who worked the fly towers were sailors. Perched as they were on their high rigging, their only means of communicating instructions to each other was by whistling softly. A casual whistle from the stage could have brought down tons of rigging on the actors' heads.

Even non-thespians know better than to mention *Macbeth* — by name it is referred to as The Scottish Play. One unsuperstitious actor/director refuses to entertain the notion that Shakespeare used real witches' incantations to cast spells. 'Nonsense,' he says, but adds, 'nevertheless an astonishing number of actors have been killed or injured during the Scottish Play.'

Backstage camaraderie is warm and real. Actors become a close-knit, exclusive unit for the run of a play (or film). Even beginners and junior cast members are automatically on first name terms with the leading players. But no matter how close the backstage friendship there is total respect for privacy in the performance area, theatre etiquette recognising the need for personal stillness before a performance.

Opera, Ballet, Concerts

As with theatre, punctuality is the essential virtue. It is not only a virtue but a necessity, as entry to the auditorium is prohibited once the performance has started. An early arrival at the Opera House or Concert Hall is the first essential, and, as with the theatre, it is advisable to order drinks before the performance.

One goes to opera for the music and the spectacle. Understanding the story-line, which is usually highly convoluted, is unnecessary. Yet a British best-selling author and his wife disturbed a whole row by leaving in the middle of a performance during the Wexford Festival because the opera was in Italian and they didn't understand a word. Music has no language barrier. The management frowns on an over-enthusiastic desire to enter into the performance by singing or humming along with the singers. For the audience it is also singularly irritating to sit beside an amateur conductor at a concert, who waves his imaginary baton in the air. A formidable Dublin dowager put a stop to just such a distraction by leaning across and saying, 'The conductor seems to be managing quite well on his own'.

SHOWING APPRECIATION

Regarding applause, be prepared to clap enthusiastically every time the figure in white tie and tails dashes in from the wings — he is the conductor. Unless familiar with the score do not applaud during a performance, let the rest of the audience lead the way. Many a lone clapper has mistaken the end of a movement for the end of a piece. Enthusiasm can be vocal — it usually is in Italian opera houses — but be sure to get the gender and number right when shouting *Bravo*. *Bravo* is singular male, *Brava* singular female, and *Bravi* plural.

Performances in great opera houses of Europe are partisan affairs. Singers have their individual claque (a hired body of applauders) who are equally prepared to 'Boo' rivals as they are to *Bravo* their own favourite. At the end of a performance they can be found tossing bouquets on to the stage. A more formal admirer sends flowers backstage, making sure the accompanying card is firmly attached.

AFTER THE PERFORMANCE

Performers welcome a visit backstage from friends, before they lose their high and exhaustion sets in. Praise cannot be too lavish or too prolonged. As Alan, star of stage and the small screen, explains, 'We do not need to be told how bad we were, we already know that'. The worst of all is bitchy praise, especially when delivered by a fellow thespian. As the actress said to the mother of the young star at the première of a major feature film, 'I don't know what they are all talking about, I thought your son was rather good'.

There is an unwritten code of behaviour which makes it unacceptable to ask an artist to perform when they are a guest at a private party. Many a time the artist, if in the mood, will sing, dance, play or recite, and generally give their all. That is their option. It is also unwise to mix business with pleasure. A professional when playing at a private function may prefer to get on with the job and leave. It is no great favour to them if a celebrity-seeking hostess insists that they join her guests for dinner. As a famous American hostess discovered when she hired a professional musician to play for her guests. 'I will expect you to join us for dinner,' she graciously commanded. 'In that case Madam my fee is doubled,' was the reply.

Dealing with
Celebrities

There are two types of celebrity — the one who after years of effort in some form of activity has come to public acclaim, and the overnight celebrity who becomes a household name but nobody is too sure why. There is of course a third type, a notorious celebrity such as a serial killer or major terrorist. We shall leave such people to the care of law enforcement agencies.

Dealing with the first category should be a straightforward matter. Their V.I.P. status stems from achievement in their chosen field and as they usually associate themselves with events pertaining to their own area, looking after them at functions is made relatively easy through mutual interest. The occasion could be a scientist inaugurating a new research laboratory, an actor opening a drama season, an author at a book signing, an artist being honoured, a singer awarding prizes, or a T.V. personality opening a shopping centre. If the V.I.P. consents to appear and perform at the function, sheer professionalism and good manners should carry them through.

Massive egos can cause some sticky moments and such a one occurred when an internationally-known actress with a notorious family life agreed to attend the Dublin première of her latest film. An important part of the evening's entertainment was the onstage interview to be given by various V.I.P.s connected with the film. The producer, director, writer and other stars ran through their interviews effortlessly, but the actress turned in a fey monosyllabic performance. It was embarrassing for the interviewer as well as the audience. V.I.P. status brings with it some responsibilities — good manners are not the least of these.

Speaking in Public

There is a happy medium between monosyllabic and verbose. An organiser will usually suggest a time limit for a speech and this is ignored at one's peril, particularly if the listeners are on their feet. No matter how erudite and witty the speaker it really is difficult to retain concentration and a sense of humour while standing.

It should not be necessary to mention that the greatest insult to offer an audience is to patronise them. Too frequently celebrities will do just that by unconsciously belittling the occasion. They may do this by referring to the amount of times they have to perform this same function. Any V.I.P. worth their salt will give the impression that the present ceremony is as important to them as it is to their audience. At a graduation ceremony recently in the U.K. the unknown V.I.P. officiating let his audience know the difficulty he had in bringing a fresh speech to each of these ceremonies. The majority of his listeners had travelled for miles to see their offspring receive their just rewards and were uninterested in an unknown celebrity's speech-writing problems.

Autographs

Most celebrities can write and have no objection to signing their name for admirers. But there is a time and place for everything. A film première, book signing, first night, exhibition-opening or other public function could be considered suitable occasions to request an autograph. Ireland's best-known poet was once asked to sign an autograph after a performance by a Russian ballet company and to this day he wonders did the fan confuse him with one of the Bolshoi dancers. Then there are the private moments in public places, unsuitable for autograph hunters, such as while eating with

friends in a restaurant, or checking into a hotel with someone else's partner — it has happened! Too much attention is almost as off-putting as too little.

Celebrities' Egos

It should be remembered that V.I.P. status does not come with a suit of armour, except in the case of politicians. Artists who depend on public acclaim are sensitive to the point of rawness. When meeting them therefore, bear in mind the golden rule — praise unstintingly and if you cannot do that, stay quiet. It is impossible to go over the top with praise.

A leading politician in this country had just finished a not very amusing anecdote describing how he had routed the opposition. As he sank into silence his wily girlfriend said breathlessly, 'Tell me again'. Without hesitation, he retold the story. Which just goes to show that over-the-top is not an applicable term when measuring praise for performers.

Anything that is not outright praise can be deemed adverse when you are dealing with egos of this size, even a quibble about the acoustics or the seats will be taken personally. One such sensitive soul was a theatre director who bristled every time 'his' theatre was mentioned. Cecil regarded himself as rather an expert on the director's job. During a luncheon party in the house of mutual friends, Cecil took it upon himself to let the director know where he was going wrong. Our sensitive theatre man was upset, the hosts were furious, the guests uncomfortable. An awkward moment that good manners would have avoided.

If one happens to hate the work of a visiting celebrity it is best to keep one's counsel as there are thousands of ways of pricking an ego surreptitiously. In public, if one has nothing good to say, say nothing. Adverse opinions are acceptable only from those who are paid to deliver them, and that still does not make critics welcome in some circles.

Equal only to amateur critics in terms of thoughtlessness are unbelievers. These are the people who believe that artists do not 'really' work. 'I know you are a pianist,' announced one such philistine, 'but what do you really do?' The concert pianist in question was unfailingly polite as he explained that as well as a heavy touring schedule he had recording dates, master classes, judging at competitions and hours of practice to get through every day. His listener was impressed. 'Let me shake your hand' he said. This he proceeded to do with such enthusiasm that he broke the pianist's finger.

Beware the celebrity who declares, 'Just treat me as an ordinary person'. The message they are often conveying is quite the contrary. If things go wrong they can easily lapse into 'Do you know who I am?' Of course there are people upon whom fame has had no adverse effect. They are a pleasure to deal with.

Andy Warhol hit the nail on the head when he said that everyone has their fifteen minutes in the limelight. But even such a short exposure can cause permanent damage, not unlike the temporary blindness after the bright flash of a camera. The status of celebrity can bring with it many good things, but it is wise to bear in mind that it is not permanent. There are others beavering away below to reach the same plateau, and the higher one climbs the less attractive one's rear becomes to those below. Fame very often comes through the media. However what journalists bestow, journalists can take away, and as clear as night follows day, they will. Today's fashionable figure is obsolete tomorrow and it is well to bear that in mind when in the limelight and employ perfect politeness at all times. Fame is short but memories are long.

There was an amusing incident in a recent film where one of the heroines thought U2 was a submarine. It is wise to bear that in mind when publicly introducing a celebrity. The lazy cliché, 'X' needs no introduction, should be avoided as 'X' could well be a mystery to the audience.

Basking in another's limelight can lead to withdrawal symptoms when the star expires. Using a V.I.P. for personal elevation should be done with the maximum of discretion, otherwise one could be termed an opportunist. Many a home is filled with photographs of the owner with the man or woman of the moment, a photographic legend of their career. Obtaining this memorabilia is an enjoyable challenge for those who have no fear of appearing pushy. But there is an easier method of filling one's walls with irrefutable documentary evidence of closeness to V.I.P.s without having to draw one unctuous breath. One witty wine correspondent hit upon a clever notion. He took his camera into Madame Tussaud's (in London) and had his photograph taken posing beside kings, queens, and heads of state. Whereas the wax effigies might have looked a little false in real life, on film they are most convincing.

Travel Etiquette

Nowhere is the acceleration of the pace of life more apparent than in the means and method of travel. We shall look mainly at air travel, as today's frequent flyer is the rule rather than the exception.

As recently as the Eighties I was witness to the following conversation in Palm Beach. A renowned, non-wage-earning yachtsman in his mid-fifties joins a group of friends for dinner, it being clear from his manner that he has some important news to impart. 'Guess what,' he says, 'I've just flown commercial.' The statement is greeted with murmurs of surprise and curiosity. 'The extraordinary thing is,' he explains, 'that even in first class, they put you sitting beside people you don't even know.' Shocked surprise!

In a world of apex fares, seasonal reductions, travel miles and a general sensation of flying in a mobile cattle pen, there are still some people for whom travel was once a pleasurable leisure occupation. No doubt in such gracious circumstances politeness was a way of life. However, with over-crowded airports, stations and roads, impatience can boil over making it appear that good manners is a leisure occupation. This is the very time when good manners are essential for sanity. Universal politeness could put the pleasure back in travel.

Air Travel With Children

Robert Benchley would divide travellers into two groups: first-class and those with children. This is one of life's truisms. Warm feelings for cuddly babies disappear when seated beside an unhappy one for a long flight. Ian found this to be all too true. He would have regarded himself as being at least tolerant of children. For the first hour or so of the flight he accepted the occasional kick as the ill-luck of the draw, but when two untouched drinks ended up in his lap, he suggested that he might be seated elsewhere for dinner. Instead of the upgrading he hoped for he ended up on the crew jump seat with barely space to move his arms but at least his tray was secure. The baby's mother had done her best within the confines of the allotted space.

There is a growing school of thought in favour of a separate children's section, to reduce the strain on parents, children, and other passengers. Passengers who prefer to avoid children now frequently check into the smoking area, feeling that a caring parent would not subject their offspring's little lungs to the pollution — rather a high price for a non-smoker to pay.

Some children are perfect passengers being naturally placid or very well-behaved. Theirs are the parents armed with bags of toys, and games for the journey. These little angels can even get through the flight without a trip to the lavatory every ten minutes. Conversely, there are parents who regard the aircraft as a playground and the flight attendants as nannies, and naturally their little ones act up. Some desperate parents resort to administering tranquillisers as a short-term solution. This is risky — better one nightmare journey than a lifetime's substance dependence. Frankly babies are too young to understand consideration for others, especially as their ears block on take-off and landing. However their slightly older siblings can learn to consider their fellow passengers.

Aircraft Baggage

Hand baggage on an aircraft is both reasonable and acceptable when carried by oneself but excessive when toted by others. Airlines differ in what they permit, albeit that there is an internationally acceptable size of on-board travel bag. One certainty is that the heaviest bags are destined to be loaded on top of crushable coats. One solution to this is to sit tight until airborne and then stow coats overhead. Baggage can be a serious cause of conflict between crew and passengers; the answer lies with the airlines. If luggage was unloaded as fast as passengers there would be no necessity for the majority of hand baggage, particularly if they managed to offload them at the same destination.

Sea Travel

A short ferry journey hardly qualifies as a voyage, and yet even on the briefest trip there is a certain sense of camaraderie which is lacking on an aircraft. Ships' passengers are friends until proved otherwise: fellow airline travellers are a challenge. It all has to do with protecting one's own space. Animals urinate to establish their boundaries, humans emanate waves of aggression. Quite apart from speed, space is the main advantage of ships over airplanes. The great advantage of first-class travel is that money buys even more space and greater privacy, and one long-time cruise passenger even insists that the weather is better in first-class.

Train Travel

On long journeys, train travel falls somewhere between the leisure of the boat and the hassle of the aircraft. Fellow passengers are friendly but wary. The lower the compartment class, the friendlier its occupants. One of this writer's happiest journeys was travelling third-class through Spain, where there were more livestock than passengers in the carriage and an endless supply of food, drink and advice. Wariness, and indeed suspicion increase in the more rarified atmosphere of first class. C.S. Lewis recounts that on one occasion, when looking particularly shabby, he was accosted by a formidable matron who enquired of him: 'Have you got a first class ticket?' His perfect reply was, 'Yes madam, but I'm afraid I will be using it myself'.

Travel in overnight couchettes would be transformed if all the passengers behaved in a reasonable manner and stowed their baggage in their immediate space. Woe betide the last passenger to arrive in an overnight compartment as they will inevitably find the luggage racks around their bunk are bulging with bulky bags, stowed there by the first arrivals. One irate English woman kept her Anglo-Saxon cool as she heaved the intrusive luggage out of the compartment on to the station platform. The reaction was voluble, but the result was a reasonably roomy bunk. Sleeping with strangers and their luggage takes the glamour out of travel.

Travelling With Friends

The essence of travelling with friends is compatibility. If one has a friend who is flexible, unfazed by delays, unafraid of new experiences and with a sense of optimism, then one has the ideal travelling companion.

An essential preparation for such a journey is to sort out the financial arrangements in advance. Whether it is to be a common kitty or everyone for themselves, it saves much unpleasantness later to be cut and dried about it before departure. Experience indicates that a common kitty may be easiest to handle, but Murphy's Law decrees there will always be one who suffers a temporary paralysis when it comes to putting hands into pockets. Better to extract their dues on home ground on a daily basis.

Giving one another space is important on a shared holiday. Living in each other's pockets can put a strain on the warmest relationship. A morning or a day's separation unites rather than divides and creates a natural desire for a return to shared companionship.

Whether to travel with a member of one's own sex or the opposite is a matter of personal taste, and availability. Despite women's liberation and independence, in the remoter parts of some Islamic countries, a male companion is a real boon.

Clothes and Customs Abroad

An examination of the customs of a country prior to departure, via a guide book or tourist office, can save potential embarrassment later on. It is deeply offensive to some societies to see tourists, male or female, walking around half naked. A little thought is all it takes to throw on a cover-up. Visiting places of worship also demands sartorial respect, some authorities insisting on the head and arms being covered, others requiring shoes to be discarded. Poor Ann was passionate in her love of India, the people, the culture, the country, but she found the 'no shoes' rule in certain places hard to take. What got to her was listening to the wracking coughs and knowing that the results would shortly be spat out at her feet. Quite literally it made her toes curl. She followed the rules but with a great sense of distaste.

There are places which frown upon trousers for women. This reminds me of the stories told of Scottish forces during the Thirty Years War. When they marched across the German border, bagpipes wailing and kilts flying, the brave German soldiers downed their weapons and fled in terror. They reasoned, 'if these are the women what will the men be like?' However, it is rare these days that entrance would be forbidden to a lady in pants, but if in doubt — check.

The same applies to ties and jackets for men. One pretentious hotel in the mountains of southern France refused entry to a party of four to the bar because two of the men were jacketless. The third man had a modish collarless buttoned tunic which was acceptable, the woman wore a silk shirt. The jackets supplied by the hotel, from a selection in their hall wardrobe, were tight and uncomfortable. Keeping up standards is one thing, petty rules are another; only the finest hotelier can walk the fine line.

We have just discussed what suits others. Now let us examine clothes worn in the name of self-interest. Loose, layered clothes for travelling, particularly flying, are the answer. But always bear in mind that only the better-dressed passengers are elevated on an aircraft — the sloppy never get an upgrade. One frequent transatlantic traveller was upgraded but once — when she wore a hat. Of course, paying first class passengers can look like scarecrows if they want. The secret is to look good and be comfortable at the same time. Shoes play a major role here, a good tip being to pack at least one pair of shoes a full size larger than usual for comfort. There is nothing more unattractive than a pinched expression from pained feet.

Tipping

Remuneration should reflect the standard of service. Bear in mind that the word 'tips', which is said to have originated in the taverns of Elizabethan England, is an acronym for 'To Insure Prompt Service'.

Giving a tip in error often causes embarrassment, if, for example, the owner of the establishment is mistaken for an employee. In Mary's case it was the ducal owner of one of Britain's finest stately homes. She handed him a modest sum for carrying her baggage upstairs and when introduced to him a few minutes later she wanted to bolt instantly. His Grace, on the contrary, was delighted, said it was the 'easiest few bob' he had ever earned. The message here is that recipients are really not embarrassed by being tipped.

As regards tipping while travelling, the practice varies according to the mode of travel. Airline stewards are not tipped, whereas ship stewards are, but never the officers. Seasoned travellers often tip on the first day and they are easy to detect as they are usually surrounded by unctuous attendants. Some (very few) ships specify 'no tipping'. This is a boon to passengers as many would prefer the overall cost of the voyage to be increased rather than to have to scatter envelopes of cash around the ship like bridal confetti. The recipients of largesse are the cabin attendants, dining-room waiter and head waiter, bar steward, games and leisure organisers, beauty parlour operators and deck attendants. There is a standard rate expected, and travel agents or fellow passengers are the best advisers, or one can take a chance and judge the acceptability of the sum by the manner in which it is received.

Tipping on trains follows the same pattern, although the sum given does depend on the duration of the trip; once again the night attendants and restaurant waiters have to be looked after. The tipping of porters is a separate matter which shall be dealt with later.

TIPPING IN HOTELS AND RESTAURANTS

Tipping in the United States has reached epidemic proportions; in luxury hotels and restaurants it is now a serious budgetary consideration. The rule appears to be, if it moves, tip it. Good service warrants a tip. Doing one's job adequately or indifferently hardly merits a reward, yet custom dictates that all should be tipped, the given sum representing the degree of satisfaction. Some of us have a problem with this, but just have not got the guts to protest. Then again in today's work-intensive society, many a willing if incompetent attendant could be a son or daughter in seasonal service. Wages in the service industries are often low, making the staff dependent on tips: withhold a tip and they could be on the breadline. Emotional blackmail maybe, but then that is what tipping is about.

Arrival at a top hotel requires a wad of notes. First there is the doorman, who opens the door of the taxi — the reception and check-in area is a tip-free zone — next comes the porter who shows one upstairs. Unless he also carries a case he is followed in quick succession by another porter bearing the luggage. Every call on room service necessitates a tip. Most guests like to leave a sum also for the room attendants. The same procedure happens in reverse on leaving.

Perhaps the most influential, or essential person in a top hotel is the hall porter. He can find the best, indeed the only, theatre seats available, as well as a table at the 'in' restaurant. Be careful not to hand over the tip until the service has been rendered, unlike poor Ursula whose husband had left her at the airport to join a shoot and arranged to meet her later at their favourite hotel in London. 'What if they haven't got room for us?' asked Ursula. 'Just slip the hall porter a few pounds and he'll look after us' were his instructions. Obediently she did just that. She greeted the hall porter by name, handed him a large sum, for which he thanked her but explained that the hotel was full. Ursula is still convinced that her husband would have bribed his way to a room, and well he might. It is not just the tip itself that gets service, it is also the manner in which it is given. Confidence, not diffidence wins out here.

Tipping in luxury restaurants can add another 25% to the bill. Once again there is the doorman, in some cases valet parking, and once inside, there is the coat check, followed usually by a drink at the bar and a tip. The head waiter is tipped as are the table waiter and the wine waiter, even a trip to the bathroom runs up the cost. The simpler the establishment the less people there are to remember. (For tipping in a private house, see page 61.)

Telephone Manners

Treat the telephone like a friend but do not let it get the upper hand and become a bully. It is not easy to ignore a loud insistent ringing, but if you are sitting down to a meal, in the bath, or making love, let it wait. An answering machine can deal with the problem temporarily. If the telephone is too insistent to ignore, be brief and arrange to call back later. One should never be pressurised by the 'phone. If trapped by a sudden, unexpected request, do not deal with it there and then but arrange to call back. When in doubt, buy yourself time by promising to return the call — and do.

How to Answer the Telephone

The correct way to answer the telephone at home is by saying 'Hello'. Giving out a name and number to someone who may turn out to be a nuisance caller is not a good idea. The onus is on the caller to give details. Many people answer giving their number and there is nothing incorrect about this; withholding information is merely a security precaution.

There are households which like to announce themselves as, 'The Brown residence'. Although accurate this comes across as a trifle pretentious. Whereas 'The Brown residence, the butler speaking' is positively toe-curling. Grand folk who live in big houses that include butlers, have names for their imposing residences. It is equally accurate and more pleasing to the ear for the butler to answer the telephone with 'Buckingham Palace', 'Castlemartin', or 'Fort Belvedere'. 'Twelve Sea View Terrace' lacks a certain cachet.

Tone of voice is very important as the telephone is your line of communication with the outside world; it reflects the image you wish to portray. It isn't always possible to get a smile into the voice when answering the 'phone, but easier if you force a smile on first. Irritation, boredom and indifference come across loud and clear, no need to fake them. A surly 'What?' is enough to persuade the caller to hang up at once. 'Who's that?' is almost worse. Given a chance the caller will announce themselves.

Young people are natural mimics, that is how they learn. If they pick up the receiver they are likely to say, 'Hello', 'Brown Residence' or 'Buckingham Palace', or whatever greeting they have heard used. There is an equally strong likelihood that they will say 'What?' or 'Who is it?'; even mimics require a little training. Therefore, when there are children in the house, as there is no way of preventing them answering the 'phone, show them how you would like it done. They can be a big help, except when it comes to taking messages. This poses a problem for them. It is always advisable to check after leaving a message with offspring of a household, no matter what age. Messages and children do not mix.

Children and the Telephone

Children should also be advised of the dangers of answering the telephone when alone in the house, or of giving information to strangers. For example David, who is now moving into his Thirties, could not be restrained when younger from passing on unsolicited family information to whoever called. He would happily tell total strangers, 'Don't ring back next week, we are all going to Florida for a month', or 'You could call back tomorrow, there's a big party on so they'll definitely be in', or 'Dad said not to disturb him, he's got a hangover'.

Making a Call

Callers should identify themselves, even before asking for the person they wish to speak to. This is not so essential in personal calls but it is helpful. It also means that if you enquire for someone and are told they are out, it sounds credible, instead of asking to speak with Mr Bloggs, being asked 'Who's calling?', and then being informed, 'He's out'. The tendency is to feel, he's out to you. So it is best to reply to 'Buckingham Palace' with 'This is Mary Bloggs, would Elizabeth like to come out to play?'

It is considered bad form to give yourself a title over the telephone. Mary Bloggs is too well mannered to say 'Tell your mother that Mrs Bloggs would like to speak to her'. Neither do members of the professions or aristocracy use their titles. Honorary doctorates are not used in either a private or a business situation. Modesty means one runs the risk of being treated casually, but surely this is preferable to standing on one's dignity — a lonely place to loiter.

Coy callers who do not give their name but try the 'Guess who' game deserve to have their telephone cut off. To put people in a spot with the egotistical assumption that one's voice is instantly recognisable shows a lack of common sense, let alone manners.

Telephone Conversations

Business calls are by their nature brief; private chats can go on forever. It is highly agreeable if the telephone rings during an idle period, offering an opportunity for an amusing gossip. But synchronised idle moments are hard to find, so the caller should ascertain if the timing is right. 'Is this a good time?', deserves an honest answer, either that it is or that a return call can be made at a time that is mutually suitable. If the time is limited it is best to say so. 'I'd love a chat, but I have to go out in fifteen minutes.'

Every telephone should come with an eavesdropper warning. Overhearing conversations can be intentional and for this a bug is inserted. However, most of us live lives removed from the cutting edge of politics or power and for us eavesdropping comes about accidentally through crossed lines, particularly with mobile telephones. Therefore using the telephone for passing confidential messages is downright foolhardy.

Speaking directly into the receiver is not the only way to be heard over the telephone. A wise precaution to bear in mind is that even when covering the mouthpiece by hand, sound leaks through, especially if one is shouting. For example 'Those ghastly Browns have asked us for dinner again, what can I say?' Even a shake of the head can be transmitted — you know those times when the caller's name is repeated loudly, only to be followed by 'Sorry they're not in'.

The Long Goodbye

An inability to say 'goodbye' is quite common in Ireland. Never wishing to appear rude or rushed means that nobody wants to take the initiative to end a conversation. Telephone calls in other countries are ended with a crisp 'Goodbye'. Here in Ireland, a warning note is sounded towards the end of a conversation with 'I'd better say goodbye'. This is the cue to launch a new topic on the line, or to start the long wind down with an 'Ok so' and 'alright then' followed by a litany of 'see you', 'take care then', often completed with a religious invocation such as 'God Bless'.

The polite way to get off the line is a pointed 'I mustn't take up any more of your time'. If the response is, 'But, I've all the time in the world', you are in trouble. However, most telephone users understand this little code. If they don't, one has to invent another call coming through, a burning roast, or a bad line. Unlike the sudden death of telephone calls as depicted in films, where conversations are ended with a dramatic slamming down of the receiver, real life calls expire gradually from exhaustion.

Business Calls

It should go without saying that business callers should cut out the preliminaries and get straight to the point. This is often easier to do with a fax where it is not necessary to enquire about family members. Brevity and clarity are the cardinal virtues. Having all relevant data laid out is essential, whereas calling someone and then having them hold on while you search through a filing system shows a thoughtless disregard for their time.

Trying to get through to a business executive can be one of life's major frustrations. As in Jason's search for the Golden Fleece there are a number of insurmountable obstacles put in the way. The first of these is the company's receptionist.

The Receptionist

One of the unsolved paradoxes of the corporate world is that whereas companies will spend a fortune on creating and polishing a public image, they will neglect their single most important contact with the public — the telephonist. Telephonists are the public voice of the company, yet they are very rarely given clear guidelines on the corporate image which they are supposed to project. Every head of a large company should try telephoning their own office, they might learn a great deal about the image of their company as perceived by the public as well as the difficulty in getting through to themselves.

The golden rules for receptionists are:

- Answer with a smile in your voice.
- Make a positive response to any enquiry.
- In case of delay, give the caller an update every thirty seconds.
- Never hold up the caller for more than three minutes. Suggest that the caller may have other things to do and take the number and call back.
- Be diplomatic, friendly and co-operative and make the caller and their company feel good.
- Do not address the caller by first name. Although first names may be part of your company's corporate culture, the caller is not part of your company. There is a story told of the actor William Rushdon being 'Willie'd by someone's secretary. 'Goodness,' said he, alarmed by the lack of reserve, 'you'll be slapping a paternity suit on me next.'
- It is unnecessary and time-consuming to enquire the nature of the caller's business if the call is going to be processed through a number of other people.

When dealing with a busy receptionist, be concise. Return their greeting, give your name and the name of the person you wish to speak to. If unsure of who is dealing with your problem, a brief explanation could be necessary. 'Good morning, John Bloggs speaking. I received a bill for catering equipment which I wish to query. Who do I speak to regarding this?' An efficient telephonist should be able to identify the person and department and put Mr Bloggs through with an introduction — 'Mr Bloggs I'm putting you through to Mr Jones who will deal with your query' — having previously alerted Mr Jones that Mr Bloggs was being put through. Oh that life could be so simple!

Unfortunately all too often one is handed from department to department, where each fresh voice asks the same questions, 'name and business?' Alas these questions are rhetorical and the answers disregarded. This is a real blood pressure raiser. A fax or letter might have a better chance of getting through.

The Secretary

Public perception of private secretaries varies from ogre to angel. The majority of secretaries are women, some regard their boss (male or female) with the protective instinct of a lioness towards her cubs, treating all untoward telephone calls as a threat. Quixotically, the more highly placed the executive, the easier it is to get through.

Into the ogre class falls the secretary of a prominent businessman who told a legitimate caller that not only was Mr B. too busy to talk to him, but so was she. Fortunately such rudeness is rare. A busy executive's calls have to be screened and if sometimes secretaries appear over-zealous in carrying out their duties, it is done from the right motives. On the other hand if a caller explains their case and creates a bond, however slight, a secretary can be of inestimable help. They can, for example, frequently deal with the query themselves, or obtain the necessary information, or arrange a convenient time to call.

The most common complaint against secretaries is an ungracious approach to outside callers. Certainly the formula most frequently used does not inspire confidence in the easily intimidated. It runs something like this. 'What company are you with?', 'What is the call about?' and the final blow, 'Will X know who you are?'

The excuse 'at a meeting' has worn out its credibility. Of course working people spend a great deal of their day at meetings, it is the abuse of the phrase that has caused it to fall into disrepute. A thoughtful secretary's response could be: 'X is at a meeting and will be sorry to miss your call. Can I give him a message and we'll get back to you?' This is still a relatively negative message but the way it is delivered should mollify even the most cynical caller, provided the call is returned. It is important that an employer indicates to a secretary how he wishes to be represented on the telephone, whether a courteous or a gestapo-like screening process is preferred.

Returning Calls and Taking Messages

Not returning telephone calls displays the same lack of consideration for others as keeping them waiting. (The author considers lateness the principal vice against good manners.) All telephone calls should be returned, if possible, on the same day. Nobody said that they have to be returned by the busy executive, but someone should return the calls. Never take a message without passing it on — better no message than a forgotten one. All messages should be written down instantly, memories cannot be relied upon.

An elderly mother-in-law enjoyed answering the telephone when staying with her son-in-law. But she refused to write down messages, preferring to rely on her hitherto perfect memory. The result was a guessing game every evening. 'Someone rang,' she would say, 'they said to ring them back. The name has slipped my mind. Say a few of your friends' names and I'll recognise it.'

Hidden among the genuine callers are some who can be termed a nuisance. Unfortunately they have very thick skins and cannot take a hint, even when Mr Bloggs has been unobtainable for weeks, they persist. In dealing with them, firmness is called for; it can be proposed that they use the postal system as a future means of communication. For example, 'Mr Bloggs is tied up with some very important projects at present, and will be for some time. Could you put your proposition in writing?'

Telephone Brinkmanship

Childish, is how the average person would describe the telephone power play practised by some leading business people. The winner in the 'who is the most important' game is the person who comes last to the telephone. In other words when putting a call through via secretaries, the secretary who gets the other principal on the line first wins for her side. Time and dignity would be saved all round if more executives made their own calls.

Answering Machines

Answering machines are here to stay. For companies who deal with international clients or people who work outside an office situation they are invaluable. The sooner the die-hards who refuse to speak to a machine accept them the better. These are the very same ones who berate you for being impossible to contact. Owners of machines find it really frustrating to come home to a series of recorded calls which cut off without a message.

A common fault is for an unversed caller to leave a message immediately after the telephone has been answered but before the tone. This means that only the last couple of words, if even those, are recorded. Callers should leave time as well as date. The owner could be away for a few days. Leaving cryptic messages such as, 'This is Jane. If you come in within the next ten minutes can you ring me', can drive a machine's owner to distraction. It goes without saying, or it should, that callers should speak slowly and clearly, and repeat telephone numbers and complicated names or places. Machines with funny messages amuse for about ten seconds but by the second or third call the joke has worn thin. Best to eschew humour in favour of a straight message.

Other People's Telephones

When a guest in someone else's house, all long distance calls should be paid for — offering to do so is not sufficient. Find out the charge and leave the money. If possible reverse charges when not using your own telephone or charge them to a credit card. Do inform hosts that you are doing so, otherwise you may well come in for some unjustified sour looks when they hear that the weather in New Zealand was perfect this morning. Some hosts leave a tacky or tactful — depending on your point of view — money box beside the telephone.

If local calls only are made, and the cost of these is negligible, it is best to mention that they were made. If the calls were numerous, some small gift would be in order. The same etiquette applies when using someone's business telephone. Long distance calls are paid for and an offer made to fix up for local calls. This last offer will probably be refused, but it is good manners to make it. It has to be said that the rich are the worst offenders here. It really is amazing that the people who declare that money is of no importance are the ones who hold on to it for dear life.

Unlisted Numbers

If someone has chosen to have their number removed from the telephone book, do not disclose it. A white lie is called for here. There is no point in admitting to having it and choosing not to give it. Best to lie and deny all knowledge.

Bleepers and Mobile Telephones

Bleepers were invented for emergency use, such as a doctor on call. They should never be taken into theatres, lecture or concert halls, or anywhere they will cause disturbance to others. If an emergency is anticipated, a seat number can be left with the usher who will pass on the message. The same applies to mobile telephones. If people only realised what prats they look when taking and making calls in restaurants and on the street, they would bury their machines.

Mobile Telephones: There are users and abusers of mobile telephones. These telephones can be the most useful of machines and the most irritating and are universally condemned by those who do not have them. Their nuisance value is mainly manifest in incoming calls. A quiet luncheon *à deux* is ruined if one person's telephone is continuously buzzing. Mobile telephones and restaurants are not compatible. They strike a strident note in a relaxed atmosphere, recreating the bustle of an office in a dining-room.

Incidental Manners
Refusals, Requests and Propositions

'A little less tact now saves a lot of hurt later.' (Ralph Waldo Emerson)

If a refusal is genuinely regretted because of a previous invitation, make it very clear when refusing that another invitation would be welcome. If on the other hand an acceptance is never a possibility make that clear also, or as clear as possible without causing too much offence. Not that causing offence seemed to worry Lord Charles Beresford (1864–1919) as can be seen by his reply to a last-minute dinner invitation from the Prince of Wales. His reply telegram read: 'Very sorry can't come. Lie following.' Oscar Wilde made his feelings equally clear when he refused because of a 'subsequent engagement'.

Giving a clear signal that another invitation, request or proposition hasn't a hope of success is not easy. A succinct 'No thank you' is brutal but crystal clear. Most people dig themselves into social quicksands with convoluted excuses, the result of embarrassment and an inability to say 'no'. A request to speak at a public event was made to Andrew. He had been warned that it was coming; he had done this gig before and hated it. This time he was ready for them. He practised ways of saying 'no' before the dreaded call came through. What did he say? A pathetic 'I'd love to'. Once you enter into explanations of your movements coupled with praise for the event or charity, you are lost.

Social invitations from people you do not wish to be with can be even more embarrassing, a polite refusal leaving the way open for them to invite again. If after the third refusal they still haven't got the message, be brutal. Ian was incapable of telling social lies and as a result he ended up dining with people he thoroughly disliked. Ironically when he failed to return their hospitality they considered him ill-mannered and then, much to his relief, ceased to invite him. The brief pain inflicted by a definite refusal is preferable to the prolonged agony of excuses.

Requests should be couched in such a manner that a refusal is possible; laying a trap is unwise and impolite. 'Do you enjoy opera?' is unfair, if an invitation is to follow. 'Would you be free to come to the opera next Friday?' is preferable. To ask someone 'What are you doing on Friday?' is fine if you have a genuine interest in how they spend Fridays. If however you mean 'Will you join us for dinner on Friday evening?', for heaven's sake say so.

Propositions are difficult to refuse without causing irreparable offence. Some people can manage to laugh their way out of them pretending that it is all a huge joke, and they are the first to appreciate it. This is a rare gift. Then there are the oft used lines: 'I respect you too much for that', or, 'I value our friendship too much to risk it'. Anyone who falls for those old lines deserves a straight 'no thank you'.

With propositions the surprise attack can sometimes work. Bruce was telephoned by a young lady he met at a dinner party. Her line was 'Would you like to come to Cornwall for the weekend?' A weekend out of the city was appealing, and presuming she had a house there he replied, 'Love to'. 'Fine,' she said, 'will I book two singles or a double room?' Floundering a bit but holding firm to his banker's instincts, he replied, 'A double would probably be more economic'.

Taxi Manners

Getting a taxi in New York is a combative sport. I have seen blows exchanged. A loud cry of 'I'm in labour' can work with overweight women, but not for James who was desperate to get to the airport.

Unfortunately, the competitive nature of the exercise when practised under duress, precludes any recognisable form of etiquette.

Once inside a taxi one can be faced with a non-stop monologue; pulling the glass across smacks of superiority, protesting that English is not your language can lead to a trans-continental guessing game. A ploy with a reasonable chance of success is 'Excuse me, I'm meditating'. However anyone interested in gossip should encourage Dublin taxi drivers who have a fund of salacious rumours.

Parking Cars

Cars can make beasts of the mildest men. Unfortunately a truly well mannered person may never get a sought-after parking space. In the rush for a spare space reticence is not rewarded. 'First there first served' holds good for elusive parking places. If however the car moving off reveals a car patiently sitting in front with its indicator flashing, it is not only churlish, but downright foolhardy to nip in before them. Some well-built, frustrated drivers are quite likely to resort to physical violence.

When parking it is important to leave sufficient space in front and behind for other cars to manoeuvre, also sufficient space at either side to open the door. Blocking a gateway is exceedingly ill-mannered, and parking on the footpath can cause havoc with blind people who are dependent on their canes.

Don'ts for Car Drivers

- Do not shove or push, it dents the car and you could end up in court.
- Do not meander from one lane to another, a car that cannot make up its mind is an irritant and a threat.
- Do not hinder the march of traffic by cruising slowly in the fast lane.
- Do not drive with your nose up the preceding motorist's exhaust, you never know where that exhaust has been.
- Do not shout or honk at innocent pedestrians, especially the elderly.
- Do not salute fellow motorists with one or two stiff fingers, no matter what the provocation.
- Do not pick your nose in the car. You are in a goldfish bowl. As soon as a motorist raises his hand to his face he has the attention of every road user.
- Do not make a secret of your plans to turn or stop.
- Do not drive when drunk — this is not a question of manners but morality.
- Do not use a car 'phone when driving; if needs must, pull over.
- Do not smoke in the car of a non-smoker, in fact do not smoke in any car without getting an 'all clear'.
- Do not expect a lady to help you find a parking space. She must be dropped at the door, be it theatre, restaurant, or private house. Chauffeurs are paid to do this, most escorts require some training.

Dogs, and Other Domestic Pets

We are not dealing here with the working dog. The working dog is a dignified animal who stays out of doors and is only visible when doing its job, which is assisting humans in the performance of some hunting ritual.

We are talking here about domestic pets, be they cats, dogs, pot bellied Vietnamese pigs or pythons. All animals should be trained for the life they lead. If they are permitted indoors, and allowed to mingle with humans they must develop some sense of manners. Wet patches, dirt on carpets and furniture may be quite acceptable to owners, but owners' guests may not feel the same way. Neither should over-sexed animals be permitted to attach themselves to visitors, or stick wet noses up their skirts. There is no point in the owner exclaiming with delight 'Rover seems to have taken quite a fancy to you' if the feeling is not mutual. Poor excited Rover must be banished to another part of the house.

Most animal owners do not even notice how unwelcome their pet's attentions are, especially cat owners. The world is full of people who do not care to be clawed, or jumped on, any more than they enjoy hair all over their clothes, strong animal smells or fleas. As for allowing pets near food, this is both outside the bounds of good manners and good hygiene. The only polite way to deal with the unwanted pets of others is to confess to an allergy.

There is a story told, probably apocryphal, of James Molyneux (the Unionist politician) during an election campaign. As he walked up the driveway of a house he was greeted by a very friendly dog and he petted the animal as he walked into the house. The householders, being staunch supporters, pressed him to take some tea. Tea turned out to be a delicious and substantial meal, but his enjoyment was marred by the ill-behaved animal who jumped up on the furniture, and even put its paws on the table sniffing and drooling over the food. When the time came to leave, he thanked his hosts and remarked that their dog seemed very friendly. 'Our dog!' was the shocked response, 'We thought it was yours.'

House guests should never arrive with uninvited pets. Max had a splendid house in Connemara and was a most generous host, but as a guest he left much to be desired. Everywhere that Max went his two lurchers went also. They were well-behaved and slept in the car, but were also creatures of strong feelings. They took an instant dislike to Caroline's two Pekinese when they came to spend the weekend. Within minutes the lurchers had wriggled out of the car and attacked the pekes and one was dead by the time the animals were brought under control. No amount of explanations or apologies can make up for such an incident. To think it might have been a child is too horrifying.

Beach and Swimming Etiquette

Loud music, games in confined spaces, children who enjoy throwing sand in the air, dogs who eat or pee over unsuspecting sandwiches, all of the above should be barred from polite society.

Quite apart from the fact that bikinis should only be worn when issued under licence to suitable bodies, they are acceptable on the beach and by the pool for sunbathing, but not suitable gear for swimming in health clubs. The dark one-piece has become almost uniform in these places.

Knapsacks

Normally, I would not think that knapsacks had anything to do with good manners. But since being nearly knocked off a viewing platform in Turkey by a backpacker this writer has a fair idea of the havoc they can wreak. If they were confined to the backs of young travellers in open spaces there would be no need to mention them here. Unfortunately they have moved indoors and on to the backs of female fashion followers. Stores selling fragile merchandise are threatening to ban them after one backpacker, laden with shopping, turned around in Tiffany's and destroyed a highly priced selection of crystal.

Shopping

Good manners in shop assistants is good business. A little genuine attention can part a customer from their money just as quickly as the right merchandise. Good manners from a customer can turn a bored counter-stander into a helpful (and honest) assistant.

Politeness opens doors, arrogance bangs them shut. Start off on the right note; customers should begin with a pleasant acknowledgment of the sales person's presence. A smile and a brief 'Good morning' is all that is required. If browsing was all you had in mind, best to make that clear with 'Do you mind if I look around?'; if searching for a particular item, explain in clear terms without going into the family history.

All going well, this civilised encounter should end up with a successful sale and a satisfied customer. The customer may even want to share their sense of well-being with the management; at the very least they will return.

Unfortunately shopping is not always such an uplifting experience. Some sales assistants take all the joy out of it and make parting with money as unpleasant as a visit to the dentist. Firstly, they make it difficult to get their attention by a series of ploys. They either engage in conversation with a colleague or conduct a long non-business telephone call, or, sit at their desk engrossed in paperwork, so much so that the customer feels that an appointment should have been made. The customer is in the wrong if they interrupt an assistant dealing with another shopper. They must extend the same courtesy to others as they expect to receive themselves.

The disinterested sales clerk can be really discouraging, offering half-hearted assistance and unbelievable advice. Looking good in every garment in a shop may be possible for super models but the average customer has a shape and size that needs to be suited. They know this and can expect some honest help. If no real assistance is forthcoming a shopper can always ask to see the management.

Never let a sales assistant intimidate or push for a sale. If not one hundred per cent sure buy time by saying you would rather think about it. Indecision is unpopular with assistants but common with customers. A wise shopper will always remember the two maxims, 'money talks' and 'the customer is always right'.

Every frustrated consumer's delight must be the clothes shopping scene from *Pretty Woman*, where the snooty sales clerk refuses to serve the sleazily-dressed Julia Roberts. Following Ms Roberts' Cinderella-like transformation she returns dripping elegance and oozing money, displays her mound of shopping bags to the assistant and says 'Big mistake'.

It reminds me of a similar instance which took place over twenty years ago at the Motor Show in Earls Court. As a house guest of a prominent, but self-effacing, businessman I accompanied him to the show. This man did not look seriously rich, not even jokey rich, his suits being his late father's, altered to fit. His manner was gentle and his bearing stooped, almost apologetic.

We stopped at the Daimler stand — he would only buy British — where he got into one of the more expensive models. He had plenty of time to give the car a thorough examination. Nobody rushed over to serve him, they were too busy answering the enquiries of the flash types on the stand. Eventually W. cornered a reluctant sales person. He asked some questions about the car he was interested in and enquired whether they also made vans. The salesman's patronising and careless attitude made my blood boil. W. didn't even notice. He quietly ordered six cars and twenty vans. Did that change the assistant's manner? Incredulity gave way to a sickening obsequiousness and he all but kissed the hem of W.'s hand-me-down trousers. All customers should be treated equally. You never can tell when the eccentric browser will turn out to be the dream shopper.

ESCALATOR MANNERS

The lack of escalator etiquette in Ireland could be explained by the fact that we do not have commuter filled escalators in subways and office complexes. In other parts of the world necessity has invented a correct escalator usage. Those who choose to let the machine do the work stand at one side and leave the other (usually the left) free for the fast movers. Unfortunately for those in a hurry this has not caught on here; groups stand chatting right across the stairway preventing anyone getting by.

Smoking Manners

Smoking is a habit obnoxious to some and indispensable to others. A great deal of tact is needed to cater for such diversity of tastes.

It is considered bad form to smoke during a meal. Smoking between courses is practised between fellow smokers, however the true nicotine addict has been known to smoke while eating. Present legislation forbids smoking in certain public areas, most restaurant and public transport vehicles now having segregated areas. This has turned smokers into a tight kamikaze-like club that can be encountered on the periphery of smoke-free zones, grouped in doorways and corridors. This once powerful lobby has been reduced to a group of delinquents, bound together by their lack of interest in health.

Attacking smokers for destroying the health of non-smokers is a waste of time and energy. If they do not care about their own health there is no way they can be concerned with the health of others. Gone are the days of smoking flamboyance when smokers slapped their cigarette cases and lighters on the table and when lighting a lady's cigarette correctly was something every gentleman learned. The perfect performance of this skill depended on two things: firstly, after the match was struck it was held aside for the number of seconds it took the sulphur to burn away, and secondly the match was held directly under the cigarette, not beneath the smoker's chin, thus preventing watering eyes and running mascara.

One of the better aspects of smoke control is that one can now rent smoke-free rooms in hotels and smoke-free cabins on ships. It also gives non-smokers a big stick to wield. If smoke in a public place becomes a nuisance due to air conditioning causing it to drift into a smoke-free zone, non-smokers can request smokers to extinguish their cigarettes. Although perfectly within their smoking rights, smokers will usually oblige. Guilt has made cowards of them. As the power now lies with the non-smokers they should use it with discretion and be magnanimous in their victory. Consideration on both sides is what good behaviour is about.

Smoking in private houses is tricky. There are some people who cannot bear smoke in their homes, their feelings take precedence over their guests' tastes. Fair enough, provided that they warn guests that a smoking ban is in operation. That was not the case with poor Mary, who was invited to a friend's house for dinner while on a business trip down the country. Although not a heavy smoker, the pre- and post-dinner puff represented relaxation after a hectic day's business. During her before-dinner cigarette she noticed her hosts exchange glances; after dinner someone else lit up so she joined in with relief. On leaving the house her hostess walked her to the car and cut short her genuine and enthusiastic thanks for a really enjoyable evening with the remark, 'We just wish you hadn't smoked'. It was like a smack in the face. Mary was stunned but managed to say, 'If you had told me that when inviting me I wouldn't have come'. The moral here is that hosts must make their house rules clear to guests, or otherwise let them do as they will.

'A drink before and a cigarette afterwards' was once considered the icing on the cake of sexual intercourse. How times have changed! Take the case of Ann, who was a martyr to nicotine. She had just started a passionate affair with a winsome lad called Colin. In the languid after-moments of their first night together Ann lit up on a fairly regular basis and as the night wore on the ashtray filled up. In the early hours Colin padded off downstairs. 'Good old Colin,' thought Ann, 'he's gone to fetch a deliciously cool bottle of champagne from the fridge.' Not a bit of it, Colin arrived up with the hoover and proceeded to clean the ash-covered side of the bed. The affair died some time afterwards but they remained friends.

Dress

Once upon a not very long time ago it was considered *declassé* to be too well dressed. It was felt that there was something too calculated about looking 'smart', as for being fashionable — heaven forbid! If being well dressed displayed a mild eccentricity, being fashionable was downright common. Only the middle class were supposed to be pre-occupied with wearing the 'right' clothes. The upper class didn't care, after all they made the rules. The lower class hadn't got the gear anyhow, so the problem didn't arise.

Looking 'right' is not only acceptable, it is essential in today's career-driven society. Money and success are creating a larger, wealthier middle class. Some of the newly-rich have plenty of disposable income but little confidence when it comes to dressing, or looking 'right'. The first piece of advice this little manual would offer is that there is a vast difference between looking fashionable and looking 'suitable'. An individual has to decide what statement they want to make; do they want to stand out, or to fit in? If they are in show business or the media they will probably want the first option. If on the other hand, they are parents on a school prize-giving day, their children will beg them to try for the latter.

In Italy there are people whose profession it is to tatter curtains. They are paid to age perfectly good new curtains by tearing them so that they look like antiques. Isn't it amazing that it is only humans who do not increase in value with age? Tearing up curtains does not seem such an odd occupation when you think of it, after all we tear up perfectly good jeans.

A certain well-worn look is highly prized. Shabbiness is acceptable in one's self or in one's friends, but not in one's employees, according to an entry in Thomas Moore's diary for 4th August 1833. 'Drove to Regent's Park; told of Coleridge riding about in a strange, shabby dress, with I forget whom. Coleridge offered to fall behind and pass for his companion's servant. "No," said the other, "I am proud of you as a friend; but I must say, I should be ashamed of you as a servant." '

Dress for Servants

A uniform is provided in grand establishments: the very grand have their own livery. When the Prince of Wales visited his Uncle Edward at his Paris residence, he found it rather pathetic that the ex-King still dressed his servants in 'the same livery we have at home'.

Let us suppose for a moment, dear reader, that your household style does not extend to livery. If that is the case, the male and female workers can be rigged out in white or coloured (or check or plaid) overalls, jackets or dresses, during the day, but black only after dark, or livery. White gloves for serving are still employed in grand establishments.

Clothes for Daytime Occasions

Most weddings, some christenings, State occasions, fashionable race meetings and sporting events such as Derby Day at the Curragh, Royal Ascot, and Ladies' Day at the Dublin Horse Show call for the full panoply to include hat and gloves for both sexes. In the midst of all this splendour there will be the occasional body in tatters and grunge. Never mind, life would be boring if we were all perfect.

During a prolonged social occasion such as the Ascot four-day meeting, it is customary for women to wear a different outfit each day (saving their best for the Thursday's Gold Cup). One Irish punter, a racegoer rather than a fashionplate, was so disconcerted to be greeted by a fellow countrywoman on the second day of the meet with 'wouldn't have known you but for the dress', that she spent the following days watching the racing on television.

MORNING SUIT

Formal daytime wear for men is Morning Suit. This consists of a black (sometimes grey) tailcoat, grey striped trousers or plain black trousers, a light grey waistcoat (some peacocks take flights of fancy with the waistcoat), white shirt and light grey tie.

HATS AND GLOVES

Hats appear to have fallen foul of fashion despite the best efforts of the fashion industry to resurrect them each season. For men and women they add the finishing touch. On the whole, women are more hat conscious than men, some men not bothering with anything other than a back-to-front baseball cap. One woman of my acquaintance claims to find men in hats irresistible, but let's face it, the same woman appears to find all men, with or without hats, irresistible.

The hatted male removes his hat as a gesture of respect to the ladies, nowadays a touch of the brim is regarded as a sufficient doff. They also remove their hats indoors. Women retain theirs if it is part of the overall costume effect. Nobody keeps their hat on in the theatre unless they want to cause a riot.

There are some occasions when gloves are indispensable. They are: gardening, cleaning lavatories, performing surgery, in below-freezing temperatures and when attempting to look really well groomed.

White Tie

If the invitation states 'white tie' it is a very grand occasion indeed, either State, royal or one of the professions putting on the ritz. The outfit required is black tail coat, black trousers with double braid down the outside seams, a stiff-fronted shirt with detachable wing collar, white cotton pique waistcoat and bow tie, studs, cufflinks, plain black shoes and socks. Many a white tie affair specifies 'Decorations May Be Worn', so if you have them, flaunt them.

For women white tie means glamorous ballgown, jewellery and tiara (if married). It is one occasion when it is hard to be overdressed, unlike poor Kate who turned up for a black tie dinner at a friend's house in a full-length dress of ruby red satin while the other women were wearing discreet short black dresses. When introduced to one of the male guests, his opening remark was, 'My wife thought she was overdressed for tonight, but then she saw you'! As I have said white tie demands the lot, even full length gloves if it is a royal event where arms are expected to be covered. When wearing long gloves the bracelets go outside and the rings inside and they can be unbuttoned at the wrist and rolled back when eating.

If in any doubt what to wear on receipt of an invitation for an unaccustomed event, telephone the hosts and ask what is the dress code. This writer was delighted, but thrown, to receive an invitation from the King of Sweden. An inquiry elicited the information that the royal household would all be in Court Dress, long-sleeved navy velvet dresses for the women and knee breeches for the men. Male guests were expected to wear white tie and females, full-length dresses and covered arms. One particular outfit stood out, that of the queen's butler, who wore a headdress three feet high. The reason for such an oddity was that as a previous queen had been so short she couldn't be found in a crowd, her 'man' had to be made visible instead.

Black Tie

Black tie means a black dinner jacket for men and trousers with one band of braid down the seam. Some men favour white jackets — these look their best in the tropics or in high summer, or velvet jackets in black or a colour. The latter are known as smoking jackets and are less formal and really more suited to at-home entertaining.

Then again there are some men who like to dress like band leaders in coloured evening suits; there is little one can say about such a lapse of taste other than to presume that these are the same men who wear made up bowties. Bow ties are not difficult to tie, all it takes is a couple of practice runs using the leg rather than the neck. Not only do they look infinitely more sartorially correct but they produce, with the minimum effort, the maximum sensation of smugness. Just to let the world know how correct he is many a lad pulls the bow open during the evening, letting both ends dangle — not a practice the writer would recommend for people who have no need to broadcast their faultless pedigree.

With the dinner suit goes a white shirt with a normal collar and double cuffs, and a black waistcoat or cummerbund. The latter two items are terrific paunch disguisers and the more flamboyant males introduce colour and texture with multi-hued waistcoats. The shoes and socks however remain plain black; the socks should be silk and the shoes may be patent. In my youth it was said that only cads wore correspondent or patent shoes. Odd isn't it that one rarely sees either style these days yet there are still plenty of cads around? Black tie for women can mean anything from cocktail dress, to a trouser suit or a full-length gown.

FURS

The opening up of Eastern Europe and Russia has dealt the anti-fur lobby a serious blow. Citizens of cold climates have worn fur since time immemorial and they have no intention of letting in the chill because some folk consider the killing of animals for their pelt cruel. What about leather, they ask. (Actually they don't say that at all, or not that I know of. I made it up because I dislike being threatened.)

TROUSERS FOR WOMEN

Trousers are now almost universally acceptable. It is the 'almost' that is a bit worrying as some restaurants and clubs still ban them; if in any doubt — check first. The only reason this writer can see for forbidding the wearing of trousers for women is that some behinds take more kindly to a skirt.

Fairly Useless Information

- Tiaras can only be worn by married women. We have already mentioned this little rule, it is not something that is going to keep the majority of us awake at night.
- Diamonds never come out before six. It is said that they look tacky in daytime. What a thing to say about a girl's best friend.
- Do not wear gold and silver at the same time — it tends to give the impression of 'everything but the kitchen sink'.
- Getting the gear wrong for sports is a dead give-away. (If you care enough, see under Sport, page 199.)
- Sable is the only fur for daytime wear. Did you ever hear such arrant nonsense? First of all sable is one of the softest, least hard-wearing furs, so who on earth would think of wearing it for the supermarket shopping? The sable breeders, that's who!
- Leather gives way to suede or cloth shoes and bag after dark. I'll go along with that one, nothing ruins the glamour of a silk dress like a pair of leather shoes.

- Best dressed is not most dressed.
- Coloured or string bow ties for men are unfortunate.
- Grey or beige leather shoes for men are even more unfortunate.

Sport

Shooting: Guns and What To Do With Them

Guns cost an arm and a leg, and are the ultimate shooting status symbol. Top gun manufacturers are Purdey and Holland and Holland.

Personally I wouldn't go within a mile of a loaded gun even when it is pointed to heaven or earth. The following rules are well known to 'guns' but are worth pointing out to enthusiastic hangers-on.

- Never point a loaded gun at anyone.
- Never rely on a safety catch.
- Never have a gun loaded unless you are in position and ready to shoot.
- Never be in the company of others with an unbroken gun.
- Never carry both 12- and 20-bore cartridges.

Words To Be Familiar With (or at least pretend to be)

A Gun — a member of a shooting party.

A Drive — when the birds are driven towards the guns.

A Stand — is the numbered spot where the gun stands
   (Butt on a grouse moore).

Dead Birds — are known as 'the bag'.

Clothes

Ignore fashion magazines, they never get it right. The look to go for is the peat-bog-in-the-mist effect, all browns, greens and mud colours. Apparently these colours neither frighten the birds nor bore them to death.

For the feet the choice is wet or dry, those in favour of wet feet wear leather shoes or boots, those in favour of dry, wear gum boots (wellies to townies). Next comes the jacket — the classic Barbour is ideal, but only one that is well broken in. Gore-tex is popular also as it is lighter and more pliable than wax. Sheepskin is too unwieldy for the guns but keeps the spectators happy. Then there is the classic tweed which is worn by the same masochists who opt for leather shoes; tweed takes for ever to dry. On the head a cap or brimmed hat — the brim prevents rivers of water from running down the neck. And finally the essential gloves or mitts — frozen fingers on the barrel of a gun are lethal. There are enough optional extras to keep the Christmas stocking filled for years — cartridge belts, shooting sticks and hip flasks to name but a few.

Hunting

WORDS TO KNOW

Cap — the fee that is paid over to the Master or Hunt Secretary for the day's sport.

The Master of Hounds — a very important person. He gets to wear a pink coat, and the right always to be first (almost as good as always being right). Nobody dare come between the Master and his hounds.

Hounds — the baying bunch of dogs known as a pack of hounds.

Pink Coats — these are actually red riding coats called pink after Mr Pink, the long dead London tailor who made them. They always remind me of Christmas, perhaps because they inevitably match the wearer's complexion. They are worn with great aplomb to Hunt Balls, the hunt colours on the collar. The Master may also graciously bestow the wearing of colours on senior hunt members.

Blooded — Novices are frequently dabbed with fresh blood from the fox's brush (tail). Surprisingly, this is not a punishment but is considered an honour.

Tally Ho! — Even non-hunters recognise this cry, but do they know it means that the fox is in sight?

CLOTHES

If not one of the hunt officials the correct gear is: shirt, white or cream stock, dark jacket with matching waistcoat, buff or white breeches and plain leather boots. The final essential is a hard hat, just like motor cyclists wear. The hat is not quite the same but the terrifying principle is. Hats play a prominent social role as they are constantly touched by their male wearers in greeting, handshaking and social kissing but are not really feasible when mounted.

Sailing

The first point the author would venture to make about sailing, speaking purely from personal experience, is that all skippers are bullies. The poor visiting sailor is completely at their mercy as incomprehensible orders are barked — half of them lost in the wind. The guest is supposed to leap around the boat doing all sorts of finger-chapping things with ropes and at the same time avoid the boom — a skull splitting piece of wood that runs right down the centre of the boat. Women are all too frequently banished to the galley to rustle up a meal under the most appalling conditions. The food so painfully prepared is then gulped down without a word of appreciation.

WORDS TO KNOW

Bilge — this is what the writer is sent to pump out, but is not sure what exactly it is.

Head — the minuscule lavatory where everyone shouts at you when you fail to understand its complicated pumping system.

Bunks — the narrow uncomfortable beds where nausea takes over.

Galley — hell's kitchen.

Deck — where you run around but never get the opportunity to sunbathe.

Port and Starboard — these signify left and right, but as the boat keeps turning around it is hard to know where you are.

CLOTHES

Waterproofs are necessary for the galley as well as the deck. Deck shoes — only rubber-soled shoes are permitted onboard, in order to protect the deck, their secondary purpose being to prevent the wearer sliding overboard.

Trousers and sweaters — forget glamour, nobody looks at you, they are all too busy.

Tennis

Tennis is a game where you cannot bluff. It is a bit like being pregnant, there is no in-between. A tolerant partner in tennis, as in bridge, can make all the difference, it can even turn a match into a game. Neither a cheat nor an apologiser be. Why players cheat in tennis is a mystery, their duplicity is plain for all to see. A continuously cheerful apologiser can drive even the most gentle of partners to murder.

Clothes — whites still look best; the tennis court is not the place for transparent undies.

OFFICIALS

Umpire — this man (they always seem to be men) is seated on a high chair at the edge of the net. He barks out the score as the points change. Information invisible from his elevated position is provided by linesmen. His job resembles rather that of an unarmed U.N. official in a war zone.

Linesmen — as already mentioned they check whether the ball falls within or without the play area. If out, they shout 'Fault' with all the self righteousness of a born-again preacher on the American Bible Belt. Some players insist that it is a job given only to those with impaired vision.

Ballboys — these are the 'gofers' of the game, they are the valiant souls who remain in a constantly crouched position, darting to the net in between bullet-like services. Can only be recommended for those with supple spines.

Sex — sex has nothing to do with the game. I merely bring it up to point out that the above positions appear to be exclusively male. They are rather. Leave monitoring tennis to the men most feminists might say, and give us politics, the armed forces and the church.

WORDS TO KNOW

Love — means nothing (told you it was a male dominated game!), or nil.

Deuce — is an impasse, or a draw, as both players reach forty points.

Advantage — this is given rather than taken, to the player who scores after deuce. If followed by another winning shot the game is theirs, otherwise it is back to deuce.

Golf

'If you watch a game, it's fun, if you play, it's recreation, if you work at it, it's golf.' (Bob Hope)

A golf course is where men conduct business and women play golf.

WORDS TO KNOW

Fairways — the areas of short tufted grass.

Greens — the smooth grass with the hole in the middle (only golfing shoes can tread here; letting a dog pee here is a reserved sin).

Tees — the tiny mobile platform the player drives from.

Rough — the magnet-like area that attracts the ball.

Handicap — this is not a physical disability but the shots given to level the players. One book on golfing etiquette states, 'Never pretend to be better than you are'. Golf is the one game where everyone pretends to be worse than they really are. It has to do with handicaps and gambling — or so I'm told.

Fore — what you shout when your ball is in line to land on another golfer.

Par — the number of strokes the player is supposed to take, but rarely does.

Birdie — this is not hitting a seagull but getting a hole in one.

CLOTHES

Men wear the oddest colours on the golf course, checks, plaids and all sorts of leisure shades. Trousers or accommodating skirts are de rigueur for women. Both sexes wear golf shoes, warm socks (into which trousers are never tucked), caps, and wind and rain-proof jackets.

Racing

'Everyone knows that racing is carried on chiefly for the delight and profit of fools, ruffians and thieves.' (George Gissing)

Money is an important aid to enjoying a race meeting. We are not talking here of breeders, owners, trainers, or jockeys, but of the average racegoer. There is nothing like putting money on a horse to concentrate the mind.

WORDS TO KNOW

Paddock — where you go before each race to watch the horses parade inside and the fashionable parade outside.

Boxes — where free food, drink and seats are supplied to people who can easily afford to buy them.

Bookies — like all men they promise you the earth but leave you with nothing.

Tote — the same applies to the State-run tote, except that they are more modest in their promises.

CLOTHES

The full ensemble including hat and gloves if it is a fashionable meeting. Warm sludge-coloured clothes for a Point to Point.

Rugby

Rugby is for fanatics who understand the rules of the game. Some young women go along to watch their heroes get their teeth knocked out and attempt to avoid serious injury while inflicting the maximum damage on the opposing side.

WORDS TO KNOW

Hooker	Maul
Loosehead	Scrum
Tighthead	Put–in
Ruck	Cover

There is no need for the casual spectator to know the meaning of these words. I merely draw your attention to the fact that they are genuine rugby terms and your companion is not 'talking dirty'.

All Blacks — this is not a racist slur, or description of complexion conformity, rather the colour of the jerseys worn by the New Zealand team.

Springboks — the South African touring team are quaintly named after these fine-boned, delicately balanced gazelles.

Referee — this powerful and lonely position is, according to most spectators, awarded to men ignorant of the game, with impaired vision and a fondness for whistle blowing. 'Well spotted Ref' is not always accepted as helpful encouragement from the stands.

Selectors — according to the spectators, an uninformed group with strong provincial ties, who, together with the referee, are responsible for any or all of the mishaps of the game.

Rugger Bugger — a genetic, but physically misleading term for enthusiastic followers of the sport.

Alickadoo — the backbone of rugby clubs, a more mature version of the above. Frequently known to instruct players, referees and selectors from the stands. Self-appointed custodians of the sport.

WHAT TO WEAR

The team are daintily kitted out in matching knicks and vests. Male spectators tend to dress for comfort rather than to make a fashion statement, acceptable gear being warm coats, anoraks (if you must), Barbour or sheepskin jackets (county spectators) and caps (not of the baseball variety).

Females in identical clothing and carrying rugs are usually either married to, or the mothers of, enthusiasts. Those in light-weight, figure-hugging ensembles, worn with high heels and fake tans, are unattached supporters of the players rather than the sport.

When All Else Fails — the Put-Down

Manners breed manners. In other words, well-mannered people invite politeness in return. This is how life should be, but life is not always perfect. When good manners fail to impress, the first recourse is to silence, the most perfect expression of scorn. If that fails and one has to fall from the high plateau of the exquisitely well behaved — fall with grace.

The following put-downs illustrate how to get even with style. It must be remembered in polite society that the put-down is the last resort, the ammunition held in reserve for when all else has failed.

Some of the following quotes are original, for the others I am indebted to: *In His Anecdotage* and *Theatrical Anecdotes* by Ned Sherrin, *The Oxford Book of Literary Anecdotes* edited by James Sutherland, *Theatrical Anecdotes* by Peter Hay, *Scorn* edited by Matthew Parris, *The Bedtime Book of More and Meaner Insults* edited by William Cole and Louis Phillips. Ah! you say, sheer plagiarism. Let me counter such a suggestion with another quote from American playwright Wilson Mizner: 'If you steal from one author it's plagiarism; if you steal from many, it's research.'

First an old chestnut, but one worth repeating. Lady Astor to Churchill: 'If you were my husband, Winston, I should flavour your coffee with poison.' 'Nancy,' he replied, 'if you were my wife I should drink it.' It is only fair to counter that with one where Lady Astor comes out on top. During her first season in England, when she was still unattached, an eligible young man warned her that his family never married beneath them. 'I knew they couldn't,' was her reply, 'but I never knew they realised it.'

Again Churchill, this time sparring with Bessie Braddock, the Liverpool Labour M.P. 'Madam you are ugly.' She retorted 'Sir, you are drunk'. His final cut was 'Yes, but in morning I shall be sober'.

Another former Prime Minister did not emerge unscathed when she tangled with the House of Windsor. At one of her weekly audiences with the Queen, Margaret Thatcher noticed that they were wearing identical outfits. When she returned to her office she asked them to suggest to the palace that, to avoid embarrassment, they inform her in advance of Her Majesty's proposed dress. The palace response was: 'That will not be necessary. Her Majesty does not notice what other people are wearing'.

King James II fared little better when he tangled with an Irish woman. Following the Battle of the Boyne he fled post-haste to Dublin. There he complained to Lady Tyrconnell: 'Madam, your countrymen have run away.' Her ladyship replied, 'Your Majesty seems to have won the race.'

The truly clever riposte is one that turns the insult back on the sender. Here are two fine examples. Richard Whately (1787–1863) was the highly tolerant and ecumenically-minded Archbishop of Dublin. A young nobleman who was aide-de-camp to the Lord Lieutenant made the mistake of assuming that a scoff at the Roman Catholic bishops would be acceptable. 'My Lord Bishop,' said the aide-de-camp, 'do you know the difference between a Roman Catholic bishop and a donkey?' 'No,' said the Archbishop, 'do you know the difference between an aide-de-camp and a donkey?' 'No' said the aide-de-camp. 'Neither do I' said the Archbishop. Another member of the cloth noted for his *bons-mots* was the essayist Sydney Smith. He made a devastating response to a posturing squire with whom he was out riding. Said the squire: 'If I had a son who was an idiot, I'd make him a parson.' Replied Smith: 'Quite so, though I see your father was of a different opinion.' Less elegant but equally effective was the put-down delivered by U.S. Congresswoman Millicent Fenwick to a male colleague who patronised her with: 'I've always thought of women as kissable, cuddly, and smelling good.' Ms Fenwick replied, 'That's what I feel about men. I only hope you haven't been disappointed as often as I have'.

Snobs leave themselves wide open to the killer response. Philip Sassoon was notorious for snapping up secretaryships to important people, a fact Diana Cooper could not ignore. One Easter she sent him a telegram announcing 'Christ has risen and will shortly be needing a secretary'. I once heard an Irish peer embarrass a young lady from Florida by declaring: 'Heavens! I knew people went to Florida, but I never actually realised anyone came from there.' Pity she didn't have the artist James Whistler's quick wit. When he was asked why he had been born in such an unfashionable place as Lowell, Massachusetts, he replied: 'The explanation is quite simple, I wished to be near my mother.'

Some of the sharpest insults are traded in the entertainment world. When Mary Anderson, a young actress and admirer of Alfred Hitchcock, wished to have some publicity shots taken, she enquired of the great director, 'Which do you think is my better side, Mr Hitchcock?' Hitchcock replied: 'My dear, you're sitting on it.' Lucille Ball's subtle comment on the aloof Katharine Hepburn also bears repeating: 'She really wasn't stand-offish. She ignored everyone equally.'

The famous acting family the Barrymores had great style. Ethel Barrymore managed the last word in a run-in with noisy latecomers who chattered rudely from a stage box while she was playing a scene with an elderly, slightly deaf actor. Eventually she moved front of stage and said to the offenders, 'Excuse me, I can hear every word you are saying, but Mr Cherry is slightly hard of hearing. I wonder if you would speak up for him?' The greatest of all the Barrymores, John, was equally adept at dealing with ill manners from the auditorium. When Jane Cowl, a big star at the time, attended a matinée, she chatted to her companions throughout the performance. Barrymore uncharacteristically concealed his annoyance until his curtain call when he elected to make a speech. Bowing deeply in her direction, he said, 'I'd like to take this opportunity to thank Miss Cowl for the privilege of co-starring with her this afternoon'.

Shaw and Wilde were past masters of the art of deflation. Writer, publisher and diplomat Clare Booth Luce was the butt of two famous put-downs. The first was when she met George Bernard Shaw in London during the run of her play — *The Woman*. 'Oh, Mr Shaw,' she gushed at the great playwright whom she claimed as her inspiration, 'if it weren't for you, I wouldn't be here.' 'Let me see,' Shaw nodded, 'what was your dear mother's name?' The second Luce story is the oft repeated quip she made as she stood back to let Dorothy Parker pass, 'Age before beauty'. Ms Parker swept through capping it with 'Pearls before swine'. One poisoned arrow which found a deserved mark was Wilde's riposte to the social-climbing Frank Harris, who boasted that he had visited all the grand houses of London. 'Yes,' said Wilde, 'we believe you; you have dined in every house in London, once.'

Mrs Patrick Campbell is said to have sabotaged her Hollywood career by her remark to the powerful studio head Irving Thalberg about his wife Norma Shearer. Said she 'Your wife is charming. Such a dainty creature, such tiny hands, a tiny waist, and tiny, tiny eyes'.

Overheard in the Abbey Theatre, Dublin, during a production of *Hedda Gabler* in which Fiona Shaw starred. Having watched Ms Shaw heave and flutter for over two hours, one play-goer was heard to say after the fatal gunshot sounded, 'My God, supposing she missed'.

Dame Gladys Cooper was unlucky enough to be seated beside a compulsive talker on a transatlantic flight. As she attempted to study her script the man kept boasting of his possessions all over America, his mid-Western lumber mills, the fantastic jewellery he had bestowed upon his wife, the money he would leave to his children, ending triumphantly: 'And I started out with absolutely nothing — I am a self-made man.' This was too much for the actress who leaned over and remarked: 'Which all goes to prove the dangers of unskilled labour.'

Less subtle was Alan Jay Lerner's response to Andrew Lloyd Webber's question as to why people took an instant dislike to him. Lerner replied, 'It saves time'. American playwright David Mamet doesn't mess around either when it comes to the sharp retort. He is known as a master of authentic low-life dialogue. A bum asks a well-dressed businessman for a hand-out. The businessman rejects him saying 'Neither a borrower nor a lender be — William Shakespeare'. 'Fuck you,' the bum replies, ' — David Mamet.'

Standing up to a bully is always to be applauded, especially if one can cap their insult. One evening in Paris Tommy Trinder came across Orson Welles in the Café de Paris. Stopping at Welles' table he handed him his card saying, 'Trinder's the name'. Welles snarled, 'Why don't ya change it'. Trinder came back with, 'Is that an insult Mr Welles or a proposal of marriage?' Film director Michael Winner is a man who attracts put-downs as does a betting shop loser. Missing a member of his camera crew on location, he is said to have driven his Rolls Royce right up to the Portaloo and shouted, 'If you're in there, come out now!' The voice answered, 'In a minute Michael, I can only deal with one shit at a time'.

A personal favourite is Dame Edith Evans' response to the information that Nancy Mitford wished to borrow her villa in the south of France as she wanted to finish a book. 'Oh, really,' said the actress, 'what is she reading?'

Book reviewers wield the power to destroy egos, as American critic Ambrose Bierce must have done with his one line review, 'The covers of this book are too far apart'. Groucho Marks is not any kinder about the book *Dawn Ginsberg's Revenge* by S.J.

Perelman: 'From the moment I picked up your book until I laid it down I was convulsed with laughter. Someday I intend reading it.' Equally damning is Frenchman of letters Antoine de Rivarol's review of a two-line poem: 'Very nice, though there are dull stretches.' Lord Byron had this to say of Keats, 'A tadpole of the lakes'. Unkindest of all was Sean O'Casey's description of P.G. Wodehouse as 'English literature's performing flea'.

It is impossible to resist including some of the famous put-downs by British conductor Sir Thomas Beecham. When Sir Thomas was told that a concert by Malcolm Sargent in Tel Aviv was interrupted by the sound of gunfire directed at the concert hall, his response was: 'I had not realised that the Arabs were so musical.' Then there is his infamous reprimand to the female cellist: 'Madam, there you sit with that magnificent instrument between your legs, an instrument capable of giving pleasure to thousands, and all you can do is scratch it.' Another story is told of Beecham's absentmindedness. He was greeted in Fortnum and Masons by a woman whom he couldn't quite place. Playing for time he tried all the routine questions, 'How are you?', 'How are all the family?' Still searching for a clue he enquired, 'And your husband, what is he doing now?', 'Still King' was the reply.

Sporting put-downs do not often appear in print: are they printable? Two are. The first concerns Fred Trueman's reprimand to Raman Subba Row for dropping a slip catch that led to four runs off his bowling. 'I'm sorry about that,' said the apologetic Subba Row, 'it might have been better if I had kept my legs together.' 'Yes,' agreed an unforgiving Trueman, 'it's a pity your mother didn't'. Then there is the leveller delivered to Sebastian Coe by the gate attendant. Coe was turned away when he arrived at the wrong entrance gate at Lords. He was brusquely told which was the correct gate. His fatal answer was to announce himself saying, 'Do you know who I am?' 'No' said the Gateman. 'I am Sebastian Coe.' 'Right then, you'll be able to run round all the quicker, won't you?'

Verbal exchanges in the legal field tend to be sharp. None sharper than those between judge and barrister. F.E. Smith, 1st Earl of Birkenhead, was a barrister and M.P. On one occasion the presiding judge informed Smith: 'I have read your case, Mr Smith, and I am no wiser now than when I started.' 'Possibly not, My Lord,' replied Smith, 'but far better informed.' Then there was the convicted criminal who had the temerity to address Judge Norman Birkett. 'As God is my judge, I am innocent.' The judge responded: 'He isn't, I am, and you're not.'

The pen of a theatre critic can be fatal. Dorothy Parker and Katharine Hepburn will forever linked by Miss Parker's review of Miss Hepburn's performance in *The Lake*: 'She ran the whole gamut of emotions from A to B.'

More all-embracingly damning was Peter Hammond's final line of a review panning a musical: 'I have knocked everything but the knees of the chorus girls, and God anticipated me there.' Yet another American critic, Brooks Atkins, slays a playwright with one sentence: 'When Mr Wilbur called his play *Halfway to Hell* he underestimated the distance.'

Yet it is writers themselves who make the harshest critics. The following is an example of three 'put-downs' in quick succession delivered to novelist, self-publicist and first-time playwright Jeffrey Archer by established writer Hugh Leonard. According to Leonard, Archer's play *Beyond Reasonable Doubt*, was 'the most insultingly juvenile play I've seen in a long time'. Asked if Archer had a future as a playwright, he responded: 'He doesn't even have a past.' But Leonard's sharpest blade followed Archer's revelation that he had written the play on a Friday. 'What I would like to know is,' said Leonard, 'at what time on Friday?'

Finally, there is the unintended put-down, the one which embarrasses the giver more than the receiver. Here are two examples. When Eva Peron was in Barcelona she complained that she had been called *puta* (Spanish for prostitute) as she drove through the streets. An old general, by way of apology explained: 'But I've been retired for years and they still call me General.' Closer to home is Polly Devlin's unintentional remark to her friend Diana Melly (wife of George). Mrs Melly, already an accomplished cook, decided to gild the lily by taking an advance course in the culinary art. As Polly Devlin sat sampling the first post-course meal, she enquired thoughtfully: 'Do you think it has made any difference?'

Titles and Modes of Address

The only new title that most of us have had to deal with in the last twenty years is Ms. After an initially negative reaction, it is now in common usage. It fills that gap of ignorance when one has no idea of the marital status of a woman one is addressing, introducing, or in correspondence with. If only we could have the same non-status way of addressing everyone. We have not, so it is worth a little effort to become acquainted with the correct form of address for presidents, kings, politicians, clergy, aristocrats, the judiciary and others.

Confused? Let me help you out.

Newspapers frequently use titles incorrectly, and as the majority of readers believe that newspapers are infallible, this can lead to serious confusion. Because this book is written in English the titles are given in English except where everyday usage is in Irish.

- The President of Ireland is addressed as President. There are those who like to use Your Excellency. I feel sure she/he is unlikely to object.
- Taoiseach is addressed as Taoiseach. Correspondence bears his/her own name followed by T.D., and then title.
- Tánaiste is addressed as Tánaiste. Likewise correspondence bears their name followed by T.D. and the title.
- The Ceann Comhairle is addressed as Ceann Comhairle. Correspondence is addressed to the name of the individual followed by T.D. and the title.
- The Cathaoirleach an tSeanaid is addressed as Cathaoirleach.

Correspondence is addressed to Senator (name) followed by Cathaoirleach Seanad Éireann.

- The Lord Mayor is addressed as Lord Mayor whether male or female. Correspondence is addressed to: The Right Honourable Lord Mayor (name), The Lord Mayor of (place).

I am reminded here of a little incident in Carmencita Hederman's reign. It illustrates that some people find it difficult to distinguish between a Lord Mayor and a Lady Mayoress. Alderman Hederman (as she is at the time of writing) was telephoned shortly after taking mayoral office by a well-known fashion journalist who wished to interview her about the clothes she intended to wear in office. When the Lord Mayor tried to get out of the interview, the journalist, intending to add weight to her request, pointed out that she had also interviewed the wives of both the Taoiseach and the President (the then incumbent being a man). 'Ah,' said the Lord Mayor, 'it is my husband you wish to speak to?'

Holders of Public Office

- Mayors generally are addressed as Your Worship or Mayor, or Mr Mayor. The Mayor of (place) or The Right Worshipful Mayor of (place).
- T.D.s are addressed in speech as Deputy. In correspondence as Mr/Ms (name) T.D.
- Senators are addressed as Senator. In correspondence as Senator (name).
- The Papal Nuncio is addressed as Your Excellency, or the more continental Excellency; in correspondence as His Excellency (more usually abbreviated to H.E.) the Most Rev. Dr (name).
- Ambassadors can be addressed as Your Excellency, but the more usual form of address today is Ambassador. Either title saves one ever having to learn their names. In correspondence they are addressed as His/Her Excellency (or H.E.), The Ambassador of (country).

- The Chief Justice is addressed as Chief Justice. In correspondence as The Hon. Mr/Ms (name), Chief Justice.
- Supreme Court Judges are addressed as Mr/Ms Justice, or in more common usage, Judge. In correspondence as The Hon. Mr/Ms Justice (name).
- President of the High Court is addressed as President (unless of course you happen to be chatting simultaneously to both the President of Ireland and the President of the High Court). In correspondence as The Hon. Mr/Ms Justice (name), President of The High Court.
- President of the District Court is addressed as President. In correspondence as plain Mr/Ms (name), President of the District Court.
- Judges of the District and Circuit Courts are addressed as Judge. In correspondence as Mr/Ms (name), Judge of (the appropriate court).

Roman Catholic Clergy

- A Cardinal is addressed as Your Eminence. In correspondence as His Eminence, Cardinal (name).
- An Archbishop is addressed as Your Grace. In correspondence as His Grace, Most Rev. (name) D.D., Archbishop of (place).
- A Bishop is addressed as My Lord. In correspondence as The Most Rev. (name) Bishop of (place).
- A Monsignor is addressed as Monsignor. In correspondence as The Right Rev. Monsignor (name).
- Abbots are addressed as Father Abbot. In correspondence as The Most Rev. Dom. (name), Abbot of (institution).
- Canons are addressed as Canon. In correspondence as The Very Rev. (name), Canon (name).
- Priests are addressed as Father. In correspondence as Rev. (name), (give the title of their order); a parish priest is Very Rev. (name).

Church of Ireland Clergy

- An Archbishop is addressed as Your Grace. In correspondence as His Grace, The Most Rev. (name) D.D., Archbishop of ...
- A Bishop is addressed as My Lord. In correspondence as The Right Rev. (name), Bishop of ...
- Dean is addressed as Mr Dean. In correspondence as The Very Rev. (name), Dean of ...

More lowly clergy are addressed as Mr. In correspondence as The Rev. (name).

Royalty and Aristocracy

- Kings and Queens are addressed as Sir or Ma'am, or as Your Majesty. In correspondence as Her/His Majesty the Queen/King.
- The Prince of Wales is addressed as Your Royal Highness or Sir. In correspondence as His Royal Highness the Prince of Wales. The same goes for the Princess.
- Dukes are addressed as Your Grace or Duke. In correspondence His Grace the Duke of (place). Duchesses likewise, Her Grace, the Duchess of (place). The children all bear the title Lord or Lady before their first name, i.e. Lord John X and Lady Mary X (marriage does not remove this right). The eldest son bears his father's spare title, known as a courtesy title. The eldest son of a Duke is a Marquess. The title is prefaced in correspondence by Right Hon. and is used until the bearer inherits the father's title (after the funeral not the death).
- A Marquess is addressed as Your Lord (this is a bit servile), or Lord (title). In correspondence as The Marquess of (title). His wife is know as The Marchioness of (title), or Lady X. The eldest son of a Marquess bears his father's courtesy title of Earl. The younger sons and daughters bear the same title as the children of a Duke.
- Earls are addressed as Lord (title), or the more servile Your Lordship, their wives as Lady (title). In correspondence as The

Earl and Countess of X. The eldest son of an Earl bears his father's courtesy title of Viscount. The other children are the Hon. John X and the Hon. Mary X. The title Hon. is used only in correspondence.

♦ Viscounts are addressed as Lord. In correspondence as The Viscount X. His wife is The Viscountess X, or Lady X. Their children are the Hon. John X and the Hon. Mary X.

♦ Barons are addressed as Lord or Baron. In correspondence as Lord X or Baron X. His wife is known as Lady X or Baroness. Their children are The Hon. John and The Hon. Mary.

♦ Baronets are addressed as Sir (christian name). In correspondence as Sir (christian name and surname). His wife is Lady (surname only). Their children are plain Mr and Ms.

♦ Dames are addressed as Dame (christian name). In correspondence as Dame (christian name and surname).

Irish Titles

♦ Hereditary Knights are addressed as Knight. In correspondence as The Knight of (title) on the envelope, 'Dear Knight' inside. His wife is known as Madam (family name). Their children bear no titles.

♦ Irish Chieftains are addressed as The (title). For example The McGillycuddy of the Reeks. In correspondence as The McGillycuddy of the Reeks on the envelope, 'Dear McGillycuddy' inside. His wife is known as Madam (family name). Their children bear no titles.

♦ The only Irish chieftain who does not carry the prefix 'The' is O'Conor Don.

Titles in the Defence Forces and the Garda Síochána are too numerous to list. The only comment the writer would make is that when you are in the wrong and dealing with the Gardaí, they should be addressed by any senior title or Sir!

Index